The Third House

The Third House

Conference Committees in the United States Congress

David J. Vogler

Northwestern University Press
Evanston
1971

David J. Vogler is assistant professor of government
at Wheaton College, Norton, Massachusetts.

Contents

List of Figures

List of Tables

Acknowledgments

Many people have contributed directly or indirectly to the successful completion of this research. The advice and comments of Professors Donald Matthews, Frederic Cleaveland, Thomas Cronin, and William Keech were a great aid in the planning and execution of the study. A National Science Foundation grant, made available through the Department of Political Science at the University of North Carolina, provided invaluable financial assistance.

John Sullivan and Mrs. Isabel Terry helped me to complete the data preparation and analysis. It would be impossible to list all of the others who contributed methodological and substantive advice. Parts of Chapter II appeared in *Polity,* II, no. 4 (Summer, 1970), 494–507, and parts of Chapter IV in *Midwest Journal of Political Science,* XIV, no. 2 (May, 1970), 303–20 (reprinted by permission of the Wayne State University Press).

The Third House

I

Introduction

The conference committee is many times, in very important matters of legislation, the most important branch of our legislature. There is no record kept of the workings of the conference committee. Its work is performed, in the main, in secret. No constituent has any definite knowledge as to how members of this conference committee vote, and there is no record to prove the attitude of any member of the conference committee.

As a practical proposition, we have legislation, then, not by the voice of the members of the Senate, not by members of the House of Representatives, but we have legislation by the voice of five or six men. And for all practical purposes, in most cases, it is impossible to defeat the legislation proposed by this conference committee.

—Senator George Norris

EARLY in the fourteenth century, the knights and burgesses of English Parliament decided that they could better conduct their business by meeting among themselves, rather than with their colleagues from the higher nobility and higher clergy. Thus, the latter were moved to form an upper house, and the bicameral system was established.

Bicameralism required communication between the two chambers. During the reign of Edward III, a custom developed whereby a delegation of lords was selected to confer with the House of Commons regarding the king's requests for money. From these beginnings, the conference committee as a device for settling differences between the two houses gradually developed and became a fixed institution of the English parliamentary system.

Introduced in the Massachusetts Bay Colony in 1645, the conference

3

committee gained widespread use in early American legislatures. Although the Constitution made no specific mention of conference committees as bodies for settling differences between the Senate and the House of Representatives, their use in the national legislature was assured when the Senate appointed a committee to prepare rules of conference on the first day of the First Congress, April 7, 1789. Conferences were often employed in the First Congress and dealt with such measures as the impost bill, a salary of Members bill, the amendments to the Constitution, a bill regulating the courts, the Treasury bill, and the Post Office bill.[1]

Recurring deadlocks between a mutually hostile Senate and House in the period preceding the Civil War further established the conference as a legislative institution, and by 1852 the essential elements of the modern conference system had evolved. At this stage in conference development, Ada McCown notes that

> The customs of presenting identical reports from the committees of conference in both houses, of granting high privilege to these conference reports, of voting upon the conference report as a whole and permitting no amendment of it, and of keeping secret the discussions carried on in the meetings of the conference committee, had become established in American parliamentary practice.[2]

In the modern Congress, about 10 per cent of all public laws enacted have passed through the conference committee stage of the legislative process. This figure is not, however, an accurate index of the importance of the conference committee, for included in this 10 per cent are most of the major bills enacted during a congressional session, and almost all of the appropriations measures.[3]

---

1. Ada C. McCown, *The Congressional Conference Committee* (New York: Columbia University Press, 1927), p. 39. Most of this discussion of the development of the conference committee is drawn from Miss McCown's comprehensive study of the history of this institution.

2. *Ibid.*, pp. 254–55.

3. *Ibid.*, p. 11. See also Charles L. Clapp, *The Congressman: His Work as He Sees It* (New York: Doubleday, Anchor Books, 1964), p. 286; Malcolm Jewell and Samuel Patterson, *The Legislative Process in the United States,* 2d ed. (New York: Random House, 1966), p. 475; George B. Galloway, *History of the House of Representatives,* 4th ed. (New York: Thomas Y. Crowell, 1968), p. 232; and Lewis A. Froman, Jr., *The Congressional Process* (Boston: Little, Brown, 1967), p. 159.

Conference Rules

Part of the explanation for the importance of the conference committee in Congress is found in the formal rules and procedures governing conference activity. Sixteen pages of the Senate *Rules and Manual,* fourteen pages of the House *Rules and Manual,* and twenty-two pages of *Cannon's Procedure* are devoted to conference rules.[4] The power of appointing conferees is given to the presiding officers of both houses, but the actual selection of conferees is made by the chairman of the committee which handled the legislation in each chamber. The chairman may select any number of conferees; the general pattern is to select the senior members of the committee from both parties. Since the two delegations vote as units, there is no need to have an equal number of conferees from the House and Senate.

One of the variables affecting patterns of bargaining is the secrecy of the conference activity. No minutes or written records of the conference session are maintained, and as a result the details of the negotiated settlement are generally known only by a small minority of the members of the House and Senate. In addition to the conference report, House rules require a statement by its delegation explaining the effect which the proposed changes will have on the bill as it passed the House.[5] The Senate requires no such statement by its conferees, permitting the conference report to stand alone as an indicator of the conference agreement.

A chief source of the conference committee's power in the legislature is found in the chamber rules requiring the acceptance or rejection of a conference report as a whole, subject to no amendment by either house. Because so many conferences occur in the closing days of each session, this rule has the effect of presenting the Congress with a choice of accepting the conference bill or having no bill at all. In the case of appropriations, this choice is even further narrowed by the "knowledge that there ultimately has to be a bill."[6] The enormous power which these procedures give to conferees working on appropriations measures occasioned the following suggestion by Senator William Fulbright:

4. For a more detailed discussion of the rules governing conferences, see Gilbert Y. Steiner, *The Congressional Conference Committee: Seventieth to Eightieth Congresses* (Urbana: University of Illinois Press, 1950), pp. 7–13.

5. Clapp, *The Congressman,* p. 284.

6. Statement of a member of the Senate Appropriations Committee quoted in Jeffrey L. Pressman, *House vs. Senate: Conflict in the Appropriations Process* (New Haven: Yale University Press, 1966), p. 64.

I submit, Mr. President, in all sincerity, that there is no need whatever for the ordinary, lay Member of Congress to come back to Washington for a special session.

It is clearly evident, Mr. President, that to save the world and the people of this country from disaster, all that is needed is to reconvene, preferably in secret, only those incomparable sages, the conferees of the Appropriations Committee.

From their deliberations the same results would be achieved without the expense and trouble to everyone that is involved in going through the archaic ritual of pretended legislation. It is quite clear that regardless of what the common Members of this body may wish, the conferees make the decisions.[7]

The major limitation placed on conference activity is that conferees must confine their discussion of a bill to those provisions which cause disagreement between the two houses. They may neither add new provisions unrelated to those under discussion, nor exclude or change provisions agreed upon by both chambers. The conference committee is thus conceived as being primarily a body which makes technical adjustments in House and Senate bills so as to produce a compromise measure maintaining the general thrust of the bill as it was passed in each chamber. The committee, in the words of Gilbert Steiner, "is presumed to have no mandate to decide on either the ethics or the substance of the measure committed to its care."[8]

This limitation on the scope of conference bargaining is, for all practical purposes, completely removed in certain cases. When the second house has amended a bill by striking everything after the enacting clause and adopted an amendment in the nature of a substitute, the conferees are in effect presented with two completely different bills. In such cases, Section 135 of the Legislative Reorganization Act provides:

> In any case in which a disagreement to an amendment in the nature of a substitute has been referred to conferees, it shall be in order for the conferees to report a substitute on the same subject matter; but they may not include in the report matter not committed to them by either House. They may, however, include in their report in any such case matter which is a germane modification of subjects in disagreement.[9]

---

7. Senate, *Congressional Record*, 80th Cong., 2d sess., 1948, 94, pt. 7, 9206.
8. Steiner, *Congressional Conference Committee*, p. 2.
9. U.S., Congress, House, *Rules and Manual*, Rule XXIX, sect. 913; Senate, *Rules and Manual*, Rule XXVII, sect. 3. The interpretation of Section 135 has led to some congressional discussions which boggle the mind of lesser mortals. Consider the following gay

Unicameral Legislation

As is so often the case in studying politics, an understanding of the formal rules can serve only as a starting point for the investigation of behavior. Section 135, at first glance, does not seem to profoundly affect the limits on material deemed appropriate for conference consideration. The impact of this rule on legislative behavior, however, can best be appreciated by reviewing its effect in particular instances. A case in point is the beef import bill passed by Congress in 1964.

Falling beef prices led western, midwestern, and some southern legislators in the 88th Congress to seek passage of a measure setting a quota on beef imports. Because of tariff negotiations then going on in Geneva, Switzerland, the Administration was strongly opposed to such legislation. Supporters of the quota measure anticipated that the Senate would approve a bill, but concluded that the difficulties of getting such a measure through the Ways and Means Committee, the Rules Committee, and the House floor presented a serious barrier to its passage.

The proponents of the bill devised a strategy which relied heavily on the provisions of Section 135. The House of Representatives had earlier passed a bill dealing with the free importation of certain wild animals for sale in the United States. This bill, H.R. 1839, was so noncontroversial that it had passed the House on the Consent Calendar, where one member could have blocked passage.

The Senate Finance Committee, exercising the flexibility provided by the lack of a rule in that chamber requiring that all additions be germane, struck the House provisions of H.R. 1839 and "amended" the bill by substituting provisions restricting the importation of beef. Passing

---

repartee, preserved for all time in the *Congressional Record,* 80th Cong., 2d sess., 1948, 94, pt. 2, 1739–40:

Senator X: Yet the Reorganization Act, which limits the powers of conferees, provides very plainly that conferees may include in their report matter which is a germane modification of the subject of disagreement. If the Senator will consult the dictionary, he will find that the word "modify" means to reduce, to lower to a lesser degree. In no sense does it mean that in any case the conferees shall have authority to increase benefits.

Senator Y: In regard to the meaning of the word "modify," Funk and Wagnall's dictionary states, I do not know what official status it has in this august body, but it is the only available reference book at this time: "Modify: (1) To make somewhat different, to change more or less in character, properties, form or application."

Senator X: I should like to remind the Senator that the definition says, "change more or less in character," but it also states that it is a reduction to a lower degree. I know the definition contains the word "more," but I should like to see a definition which says it can be changed more or less to a greater degree.

the Senate, the measure was then returned to the House with the bill's number being the only point of similarity with the earlier House-passed legislation. The House Rules Committee granted a rule for a conference, and a conference committee produced a compromise bill establishing the beef quotas.[10]

The strategy employed in the above case demonstrates the important effect of Section 135 on the legislative process. Senate proponents were able to circumvent the intended conflicts of a bicameral system by, in effect, skipping the House of Representatives.[11] In discussing this general strategy, Lewis Froman notes that its chief value lies in the fact that it completely avoids several legislative stages in the House: "First, committee and subcommittee hearings, consideration, and votes have been avoided; then a request for a rule from the Committee on Rules has been bypassed; and, of course, the strategy avoids an initial floor fight." [12]

---

10. The histories of this legislation and other measures illustrating various strategies centering about the conference committee are discussed in Froman, *Congressional Process,* pp. 141–68.

Representative Charles Teague, the original sponsor of the wild animals bill, lightheartedly outlined his legislative history of H.R. 1839 for his colleagues:

Mr. Speaker, a few days ago, I stood here in the well of the House and pleaded with my colleagues to be sure that they referred to H.R. 1839 as the Teague bill.

This was because I was proud to have been the father of such a clean, beautiful little fellow as 1839. Every one of you helped me in his delivery because he emerged from this body by unanimous vote. He was prepared to do great things for boa constrictors and gorillas and their owners.

But in the course of events, my little baby was sent to the Senate pediatric hospital. He was horribly neglected there for a year and a half. During all of those months he was kept in dank closets and pigeonholes.

Then, recently, some of the eminent surgeons in the Senate hospital, headed by Drs. Mansfield and Keating, I believe, decided to perform major surgery on poor little 1839.

The operation was a great success by the standards which prevail in the Senate hospital. My little fellow was completely gutted. All that remained of him was the identification number on his poor little wrist. He no longer even bore my name. His little shell, however, had been stuffed by the surgeons in the Senate hospital with all sorts of things entirely foreign to 1839, his heritage and ancestry.

This new creature was sent back to the House not bearing the slightest resemblance to the splendid little fellow who left here three years ago (House, *Congressional Record,* 88th Cong., 2d sess., 1964, 110, pt. 14, 19499; quoted in John F. Manley, *The Politics of Finance: The House Committee on Ways and Means* [Boston: Little, Brown, 1970], pp. 253–54).

11. One is tempted to imagine what the reaction of the authors of the *Federalist No. 63* would be to this strategy of bypassing one chamber. Cf. "The people can never wilfully betray their own interests; but they may possibly be betrayed by the representatives of the people; and the danger will be evidently greater where the whole legislative trust is lodged in the hands of one body of men, than where the concurrence of separate and dissimilar bodies is required in every public act" (A. Hamilton, J. Jay, and J. Madison, *The Federalist* [New York: Random House, Modern Library, 1941], p. 411).

12. Froman, *Congressional Process,* p. 149.

Use of a conference committee to mitigate the effects of bicameralism, as illustrated in the beef import measure, is not representative of the normal patterns of settling inter-house conflicts. It was presented here to dramatize the importance of the conference institution, and to illustrate the fact that conferees often enjoy great leeway in making adjustments.

When a conference committee has violated the rules governing the insertion of new material in the conference bill, a point of order may be raised against the conference report. However, as Charles Clapp notes, "Though points of order may be raised against changes of this type, they seldom are made. The subjects are complex, debate time is limited, and most legislators are willing to believe their representatives on the conference committee have done as well as could be expected." [13]

Because conference reports are seldom rejected in either chamber, members of a conference committee exercise great influence over the final wording of legislation. In a Congress characterized by decentralization and diffusion of power, "the conference committee," observed Congressman Clem Miller, "is the central core of the power." [14]

Effects of Conference on Legislative Strategies

The influence of conference committees is most evident in the final stages of the legislative process. It is not, however, limited to this stage, and, in fact, greatly affects legislative behavior at earlier times in the legislative process. Even the question of which chamber should act first on a bill is considered in terms of the conference. An administration seeking a strong civil rights bill, for instance, will benefit by the House's acting first. As Lewis Froman explains:

> Not only will the House pass a stronger bill, but the bill can then be placed directly on the Senate calendar. Also, if the bill originates in the House only one filibuster in the Senate is likely.
>
> On the other hand, if the bill originates in the Senate, there is opportunity for more delays and possible defeat. There may be a filibuster when the Senate considers the bill, and then, if the bill is to be made stronger

13. Clapp, *The Congressman*, p. 279. See also Jewell and Patterson, *Legislative Process*, p. 481.

14. John W. Baker, ed., *Member of the House: Letters of a Congressman* (New York: Scribner's, 1962), p. 114.

in the House, a second filibuster on the bill produced by the conference committee. A stronger bill usually results if the Senate is confronted with the strongest bill the House is able to produce.[15]

Another stage in which the influence of the conference may be observed is the floor action on a particular bill. The congressman or senator guiding the bill will often accept amendments on the floor which were rejected in the standing committee's consideration of the measure. By doing so, he may pick up needed support for the bill at this stage, yet maintain the legislation's integrity by quietly dropping that amendment in conference. Such action is generally legitimized by the conference committee chairman maintaining that the deletion was a demand of the other chamber and was a required part of the conference compromise.

In some cases a bill's manager may seek marginal amendments to a bill in order to have additional barters for the conference bargaining session. By packing a bill with superfluous amendments, the conference leaders are often able to effect a favorable compromise which includes all of the essential provisions sought by that chamber's delegation. Such a strategy is quite often openly acknowledged on the floor.

> Mr. President, let me say if the House of Representatives agrees to our amendments and eliminates any reduction of excise taxes, I would agree that this amendment also be eliminated. But as the Senator from Georgia has said, I think it should be open in conference.[16]

> We cannot say that the other body had any motive in mind, but I have seen this happen many times. The other body saw fit to add considerable funds for research and several other programs. When they added funds for these purposes, they also eliminated watershed protection and other items which we in the House thought very important. There were some who might have felt that they were getting ready for a horse trade.[17]

Whether a bill's sponsors seek to have a roll call vote on a particular matter is another decision which is greatly influenced by an impending conference. If they can be reasonably sure of strong chamber support, they may wish to have the roll called to record that support. A recorded vote may strengthen the position of that chamber's conference delegation by serving as a measure of intensity of support, as well as distribution of opinion, in that chamber. A senator comments:

15. Froman, *Congressional Process*, p. 156.
16. Senate, *Congressional Record*, 79th Cong., 1st sess., 1945, 91, pt. 8, 9998.
17. House, *Congressional Record*, 83d Cong., 1st sess., 1953, 99, pt. 7, 9633.

I have always felt that when one is moving to attack it is not enough to send a rifle squad up to the front, but that one should have a supporting detachment behind them.

The best reinforcement we could give to the Senators would be a ringing yea and nay vote. I am confident the amendment would pass by an overwhelming vote. Then the Senators would not enter the conference chamber with empty hands, but would enter with the massed power of the Senate behind them.[18]

Consideration of a pending conference may, in other instances, lead proponents of a measure to avoid a roll call. A close roll call on a particular amendment may serve to undercut the chamber's conferees in their argument that deletion of the amendment would lead to defeat of the conference bill. House Democratic leaders, for instance, generally avoid any roll call on the issue of foreign aid appropriations. The deep cuts made in the House are generally somewhat restored in conference, and it is the leaders' opinion that "a better result can be obtained in the absence of recorded votes in the House." [19]

Studies of Conference

This discussion has served to outline some of the ways in which conference committees affect legislative behavior. That this influence is profound is readily acknowledged by members of Congress and often discussed by students of the legislature. There remains a gap, however, between recognition of the importance of conference committees and their systematic study. Over forty years ago, Ada McCown referred to this institution as "a piece of legislative machinery which, in comparison with its importance, has received little attention from students of government." [20] Thirty-five years later, we find another political scientist observing, "Although political scientists have long written about the impact of conference committees on legislation, members of Congress believe that even many students of government do not really understand their significance." [21]

A study by Gilbert Steiner in 1950 of conference action on fifty-six bills

18. Quoted in Richard F. Fenno, Jr., *The Power of the Purse: Appropriations Politics in Congress* (Boston: Little, Brown, 1966), p. 656.
19. Jewell and Patterson, *Legislative Process*, p. 476.
20. McCown, *Conference Committee*, p. 7.
21. Clapp, *The Congressman*, p. 276.

in ten different policy areas represented a major contribution to our understanding of this phase of the legislative process.[22] Because Steiner's research focused on the period 1928 to 1948, however, it is somewhat limited in what it can tell us about conference activity in modern congresses. The Legislative Reorganization Act of 1946, to mention only one factor, has helped to create a Congress whose structure is quite different from that studied by Steiner.

Richard Fenno's admirable study of appropriations politics in Congress greatly increases our understanding of the role of conference committees in this area. The findings reported in *The Power of the Purse,* because they often differ from those of Steiner's earlier work, serve to emphasize the need for continued research in the area of conference activity.

The literature of political science includes discussions of general strategies involved in conference bargaining,[23] the role played by a conference committee in the legislative history of a particular law,[24] congressmen's perceptions of the influence of conference on legislative behavior,[25] and the place of the conference committee in the larger scheme of congressional activity.[26] A perusal of these discussions reveals that whenever there is an attempt to make general statements about patterns of conference activity, the lack of empirical studies in this area precludes the revelation of meaningful descriptive or causal statements. A book published five years ago, for example, can only tell us which chamber was more successful in conference over twenty years ago.[27] This may have no relationship to patterns of relative chamber influence obtaining in Congress today.

Part of the explanation for the paucity of research in this area is to be

22. The findings of Steiner are discussed in later chapters.
23. Froman, *Congressional Process,* pp. 141–68.
24. Stephen K. Bailey, *Congress Makes a Law* (New York: Random House, Vintage Books, 1964), pp. 220–34.
25. Clapp, *The Congressman,* pp. 276–87.
26. Jewell and Patterson, *Legislative Process,* pp. 474–82. The most recent general work on the conference that I am familiar with is that of David Paletz, "Influence in Congress" (Ph.D. diss., University of California, 1970). Some of Professor Paletz's findings are also reported in "Influence in Congress: An Analysis of the Nature and Effects of Conference Committees" (Paper delivered at the 66th Annual Meeting of the American Political Science Association, Los Angeles, September, 1970). Rather than focusing on the more common questions of "Who wins?" and "Are conference committees legislatively irresponsible?," Paletz seeks to determine how the existence of conference committees affects the nature and distribution of influence in Congress. His work represents a major effort to fill the gap discussed here, and references to his study will be made when applicable.
27. Jewell and Patterson, *Legislative Process,* p. 480. Reference to Steiner's study is found in almost all discussions of the conference.

found in the nature of the conference committee itself. The secrecy and the lack of printed records of conference meetings have convinced many political scientists to study another area in which data are more readily obtainable. Those who still wish to pursue this subject are reduced to making inferences about a closed bargaining session on the basis of recorded votes and the wording of legislation.

Organization and Approach

There seem to be two general ways of stalking the elusive conference. One is to employ a case study approach.[28] Case studies enable the researcher to analyze, in great detail, the many variables relating to conference output. In order to achieve such understanding of some conferences, however, the student is forced to sacrifice generality.

The other approach, the one used here, is to greatly increase the number of cases studied and to focus on general patterns. Such aggregate analysis does not permit the researcher to explain conference output to the extent that case studies do. In the present instance, it often resembles snapshots of a fast moving parade which show that the bands and clowns and soldiers all change position upon going through a tunnel. Because our data are incomplete, we are able to record the fact, but are unable to explain why it occurs.[29]

By dealing with a large number of cases to determine general patterns of conference activity, we hope to accurately describe certain aspects of legislative behavior related to the conference. Because of the exploratory nature of the research and the large number of variables associated with conference outputs, the present study actually explains little of the variation in conference decisions. Description of general patterns and identification of important variables is only the first step in any scientific study of

28. David Paletz's analysis in "Influence in Congress" follows this approach. Most of his generalizations regarding the conference are based on detailed case studies of the 1966 Poverty Amendments, the Traffic Safety Act of 1966, and the 1967 Congressional Redistricting.

29. The difference between these two approaches is what K. C. Wheare seems to be getting at in observing, "The student of committees has to make a choice. Either he can try to hack his way through the jungle on foot or he can try to get a bird's eye view of the terrain from the air. If he chooses the first alternative, the most he can hope for is to clear a portion of his territory; if he chooses the second, the most he can hope for is to produce a rough sketch map of the whole area" (*Government by Committee: An Essay on the British Constitution* [London: Oxford University Press, 1955], p. i).

the conference. It is, however, an important one, primarily because it describes what we hope to explain later.

A total of 596 conferences were studied. This total represents all of the conferences completed during the 79th, 80th, 83d, 88th, and 89th congresses. It was originally intended to study all conferences from the 79th to the 89th Congress. However, unanticipated problems in data collection limited the scope of the study to its present boundaries. It was decided to focus on these five congresses in order to provide a study which included conferences distributed over a twenty-year period, and to enable considerations related to Democratic or Republican control of Congress.

Two chapters deal with representation on the conference committee. Party representation and representation of supporters of the bill in conference are conceived as being dependent variables, and are related to elements internal to the House and Senate systems. Focusing on the conference system itself, Chapter IV represents an attempt to measure the output of this system in terms of relative chamber success. In seeking partial explanations for this conference output, the partisan and supporter representation are considered, along with other factors, as independent variables. It should be emphasized that while this analytical distinction is useful for organizing the study, it in no way suggests that we may consider the conference system apart from the House and Senate systems. Interdependence among the various elements of these systems is very great, and no explanation can be accurate if it does not include all of these variables.

Chapter V is a discussion of patterns of bargaining related to conference activity. By relying on the general findings presented in the preceding chapters and by studying in greater detail thirty-four conferences selected from the larger sample, it is hoped that some insights into the general bargaining process in Congress may be gained.

II

Party Representation
on Conference Committees

The Speaker appoints the managers in the House, selecting them so as to represent the attitude of the majority and the minority of the House on the disagreements in issue; and while it is usual to represent the party divisions of the House, the representation of opinions as to the pending differences is rather the more important consideration.
—Thomas Jefferson

THE IMPACT of political parties on legislative behavior has long been a subject of political science research. In contrast to an earlier period when the weaknesses of American political parties were emphasized, more recent studies of partisan politics have tended to recognize the party as a major determinant of legislative ouput. Roll call analyses by Turner, MacRae, Truman, and Froman have all demonstrated the key role played by the parties in organizing the Congress and influencing policy.[1]

This dramatic change in the evaluation of the impact of parties on legislation is illustrated by comparing two statements made by political scientists writing several years apart. In 1942, E. E. Schattschneider wrote, "It must be realized that the facts here cited prove that party control of

1. Julius Turner, *Party and Constituency: Pressures on Congress* (Baltimore: Johns Hopkins University Press, 1951); Duncan MacRae, Jr., *Dimensions of Congressional Voting* (Berkeley: University of California Press, 1958); David B. Truman, *The Congressional Party* (New York: John Wiley, 1959); Lewis A. Froman, Jr., *Congressmen and Their Constituencies* (Chicago: Rand McNally, 1963).

legislation is not very great."[2] Twenty-three years, and several roll call analyses, later, Lewis Froman and Randall Ripley conclude: "Generally speaking, the single most important variable explaining legislative outcomes is party organization."[3]

Though generally great, the influence of party on legislative behavior is seen to vary a great deal from bill to bill. Froman and Ripley conclude that party leadership will be most influential when the following conditions are met: (1) the party leadership is committed and active; (2) the issue is perceived as being more procedural than substantive; (3) the visibility of the issue is low; (4) the visibility of the legislative action is low; (5) there is little counterpressure from the constituencies; and (6) state delegations are not engaged in collective bargaining for specific demands.[4]

Some of these conditions suggest that the conference stage of the legislative process is one in which the influence of party leadership may be great. Although the first three conditions would vary from issue to issue, the low visibility of conference activity is assured by the secrecy of conference meetings and the general practice of delaying public comment until an agreement has been reached. Woodrow Wilson, one of the early critics of the insularity of conference activity, characterized it as "at best a haphazard method of compounding legislation, liable to suffer many singular accidents, and impossible for a busy people to understand when they occasionally look on with unwonted attention."[5]

Condition 5, little counterpressure from legislative constituencies, often obtains because of the low visibility of conference activity. Secret debate and the absence of recorded votes in conference make it more difficult for constituency influence to be exerted on a legislator in conference than at an earlier, more public, stage of the legislative process.

Accepting the fact that there will be great variation from issue to issue, we would, then, expect party influence in conference to be an important determinant of policy output. Because of the closed nature of conference activity and the absence of written records of the internal bargaining, there have been, to date, no systematic studies of party influence on con-

2. E. E. Schattschneider, *Party Government* (New York: Holt, Rinehart, and Winston, 1942), pp. 90–91.
3. Lewis A. Froman and Randall Ripley, "Conditions for Party Leadership: The Case of the House Democrats," *American Political Science Review*, LIX (March, 1965), 52.
4. *Ibid.*, p. 63.
5. Woodrow Wilson, *Constitutional Government in the United States*, 10th ed. (New York: Columbia University Press, 1964), p. 107.

ference output. There are, however, specific instances when the influence of party considerations in conference was publicly recognized. One such case is described by a House manager for the Agricultural Price Stabilization Bill of 1948:

> Mr. Speaker, I have served in this house for 18 years, but I have gone through my strangest and most unusual experience since yesterday at 2 o'clock. I do not believe any Member present ever went through a similar experience in legislative matters.
>
> Thursday night about 11 o'clock, the other body passed what is known as the Aiken Farm Bill. At 2 o'clock on yesterday, we were called into conference, and the House conferees to a man turned down the Aiken bill.
>
> They turned it down for the reason that they did not know what was in it. I doubt that some of the conferees from the other body knew a bit more, about what was in the bill than the conferees from the House, who had not had an opportunity to examine the legislation.
>
> At 5 P.M. on Friday we were called into conference. The House conferees, because they did not know what was in the Aiken Bill turned it down. So the conference adjourned. At 2 o'clock yesterday, Saturday, we were called back into conference, and the House conferees again stood pat and we adjourned.
>
> Then, at 4 o'clock yesterday, we were called back into conference for the third time and the roll was called, and the House committee still stood pat. We were not willing to place our O.K. upon a piece of legislation that no Member of the House conferees knew anything about, and we broke up in a rather heated discussion.
>
> Then a strange thing happened. In order to bring this conference report back, they had to rape the House conferees. When they came back Mr. Murray resigned as a conferee and Dr. Gillie was appointed in his stead; and then we met again. The Democratic Members still stood pat, but the Republican Members went over to the Aiken Bill. Now, that is the way you get this piece of legislation.
>
> Now, why did these things happen? I do not want to inject politics into this discussion, but evidently the Philadelphia Republican Convention had to have a farm program, and in order to give that convention a farm bill, they had to rape the conferees in order to give the convention a program.[6]

Although the case described above is not presented as being representative of all, or even most, conferences, the nature of conference activity would suggest that party representation in conference is a variable of some concern to political scientists seeking to explain legislative behavior.

6. House, *Congressional Record*, 80th Cong., 2d sess., 1948, 94, pt. 7, 9345.

A survey of the literature reveals that party representation is one aspect of the conference which has been discussed at some length by observers.

Minority Party Representation in Conference

Party representation on conference committees in both houses is formally limited to reflecting the party divisions in the respective chambers. Because the chairman may appoint any number of conferees, however, there is a great deal of variation in the actual proportions of party representation in conference. Some students of Congress have noted that this variation often produces a situation where the minority party is overrepresented in terms of its numbers in the whole chamber.

Bertram Gross and Gilbert Steiner independently observed this tendency, the latter considering it a problem serious enough to require reform. Gross describes the problem:

> In so far as party line up is concerned, the minority party is always well represented. The ratios usually run 2 to 1, 3 to 2, or 5 to 3.
> Wherever there is a division along party lines, this practice puts a dissident member of the majority party in a particularly strategic position. By joining with the opposition party, one dissident member can swing the balance of power.[7]

Steiner reiterates and suggests a solution:

> This leads directly to a major policy problem, the question of the distinct overrepresentation of the minority in conference activity. Minority participation in the framing of legislation is slight, but minority participation in conference is often crucial.
> It would seem desirable to increase the number of managers from the majority party. This would serve not only to increase majority party responsibility, but also to eliminate the possible unsympathetic control at a crucial point in legislative action.[8]

In order to arrive at a more general statement of party representation on conference, all of the conferences in the 79th, 80th, 83d, 88th, and

---

7. Bertram Gross, *The Legislative Struggle* (New York: McGraw-Hill, 1953), p. 321. See also Charles L. Clapp, *The Congressman: His Work as He Sees It* (New York: Doubleday, Anchor Books, 1964), p. 277.

8. Gilbert Y. Steiner, *The Congressional Conference Committee: Seventieth to Eightieth Congresses* (Urbana: University of Illinois Press, 1950), p. 175.

89th congresses will be examined here. The findings of Clapp, Gross, and Steiner indicate that overrepresentation of the minority party on conference occurs quite often and has an effect on conference output, but there have been no generalized attempts to determine the frequency of such overrepresentation or to measure its effects. To speak of a "tendency" to overrepresent the minority party is suggestive, but lacks the precision necessary to make a more general statement about the relationship between party representation and conference activity. It does, however, focus our attention on a variable which could be an important one in helping to explain conference output.

By expanding the sample to include all conferences in these five congresses and by applying a measure of party representation, we hope to arrive at a more general understanding of minority party representation on the conference committee.

An index of representation of the minority party in conference was computed for each conference committee by comparing the percentage of minority party representation on the conference committee with the percentage of minority party representation in the parent chamber.[9] The results are shown in Table 1.

Perhaps the most striking feature of Table 1 is the relatively low num-

TABLE 1

REPRESENTATION OF MINORITY PARTY IN CONFERENCE (N = 592)

	Index of Representation			
	Less than .9	.9 to .99	1.0 to 1.09	1.1 and over
House delegation	36%	38%	11%	15%
Senate delegation	47	19	17	17

NOTE: Less than .9 indicates underrepresentation; .9 to .99 and 1.0 to 1.09 indicate representation reflecting that in chamber; 1.1 and over indicates overrepresentation.

9. Donald R. Matthews, *U.S. Senators and Their World* (New York: Random House, Vintage Books, 1960), p. 273. The index was computed with the following formula:

$$I = \frac{\% \text{ of Senate (House) conferees from minority party}}{\% \text{ of total Senate (House) membership from minority party}}$$

This index is admittedly a crude one which produces some distortions in measurement, some of which will be discussed in the text. A Diogenesian search among my more methodologically sophisticated colleagues failed, however, to discover a more honest measure.

ber of conferences in which the minority party was represented at the 1.1 level and above. Only 15% of the total number of House delegations and 17% of the Senate delegations reflect such overrepresentation. This contrasts sharply with the 36% of the House delegations and the 47% of the Senate delegations in which the minority party was underrepresented. Such findings suggest that it is, perhaps, more correct to speak of a tendency to underrepresent the minority party in conference than of a tendency to give the minority party too great a voice in conference affairs.

Another aspect of the pattern of representation is illustrated by the large number of conferences in which party representation reflects party distribution in the chamber as a whole. Even when such representative conferences are narrowly defined as those with an index of .90 to 1.09, we find that 49% of the House delegations and 36% of the Senate dele-.gations fall within this range.

An objective measure of party strength on conference delegations, such as this index, cannot be used as an indicator of the intentions of chairmen in appointing conferees. Clapp, Gross, and Steiner, in observing the activities of chairmen in appointing conferees, concluded that the minority party is often overrepresented and that such overrepresentation has an effect on conference output. That this is no doubt the case in some instances is reflected in the findings of this study, but it would be erroneous to conclude that this is the norm, or that such overrepresentation occurs in most cases.

The conclusion that conference delegations generally reflect the partisan distribution in the parent chamber is strengthened when one considers the nature of the index used to measure such representation. The conference delegation always numbers less than ten members, whereas the Senate and the House have 100 and 435 members, respectively. The size differential of the two bodies compared often produces an index which suggests underrepresentation or overrepresentation when, in fact, the conference party representation is as accurate as could be achieved, given the small size of the conference delegation.

To adjust for distortions produced by the size differentials in the index, the same index was computed for each conference committee using the standing committee and the subcommittee as the base. Because the committees and subcommittees are closer in size to the conference committee, we would expect there to be less distortion than is produced by comparing the conference delegation with the whole chamber. Tables 2 and 3, respectively, show the results of using the committee and subcommittee.

Table 2 tends to verify the earlier conclusion that party representation on the conference delegation generally reflects the partisan distribution in the parent chamber. When we use the standing committee, rather than the whole chamber, as the basis for comparison of party representation in conference, we find that 52% of the House delegations and 36% of the

TABLE 2

Representation of Minority Party in Conference as Compared with the Standing Committee
(N = 592)

	Index of Representation			
	Less than .9	.9 to .99	1.0 to 1.09	1.1 and over
House delegation	30%	18%	34%	18%
Senate delegation	44	12	24	20

TABLE 3

Representation of Minority Party in Conference as Compared with the Subcommittee

	Index of Representation		
	.9 to .99	1.0 to 1.09	1.1 and over
House delegation (N = 254) *	33%	48%	19%
Senate delegation (N = 243)	37	46	17

* The smaller sample is a result of eliminating the bills that did not involve legislative processing by subcommittee.

Senate delegations reflect the party representation on the standing committee.

There is also a slight increase in the number of conferences over-representing the minority party when compared with Table 1. Where some of the variation in representation using an index based on the whole chamber was attributed to the size differential of the two bodies compared in Table 1, some of the variation in Table 2 can also be attributed to problems of measurement. The committee party ratio system prevailing in both houses is one which allocates seats on the committee to the two parties in rough proportion to the relative strength of each party in the chamber as a whole. However, the fixed ratios of the House Rules, Appropriations, and Ways and Means committees provide an exception to this rule.[10]

A fixed party ratio on the standing committee may have the effect of underrepresenting the minority party on that committee. When the conference delegation from that committee reflects the party strength in the whole chamber, the index of representation based on the standing committee ratio will indicate an overrepresentation of the minority party in conference. Thus, a conference delegation which represents the party division in the whole chamber will be classified as one in which the minority party is overrepresented in terms of its strength on the full committee.

The effect of such measurement error can, of course, produce distortions in the opposite direction and lead to a conclusion that a conference delegation is either representative or underrepresents the minority party when, in fact, it overrepresents the minority. Acknowledging the existence of such problems of measurement, we can nevertheless interpret the findings of Table 2 as supporting the observation that party representation in conference generally reflects the party divisions in the parent chamber and on the standing committee from which conferees are chosen.

The index of party representation on conference committees was also computed by using the relevant subcommittee as a base. This was done as a means of further reducing the distortions produced by the size differentials involved in the first index. The category of less than .9 is eliminated in Table 3 because none of the cases studied fell into this category. Even when we narrow the range of representative conferences to those in which the index equaled 1.0 to 1.09, we find that almost one-half of the conferences fell into this category.

Using subcommittees in computing the index of representation greatly reduced distortions due to the differences in size of the two bodies compared. Measurement error produced by the fixed party ratios on standing committees is also reduced by the fact that committee chairmen

10. Daniel M. Berman, *In Congress Assembled: The Legislative Process in the National Government,* 2d ed. (New York: Macmillan, 1966), p. 136. See also Malcolm Jewell and Samuel Patterson, *The Legislative Process in the United States,* 2d ed. (New York: Random House, 1966), p. 210; and Richard F. Fenno, Jr., *The Power of the Purse: Appropriations Politics in Congress* (Boston: Little, Brown, 1966), pp. 52–53.

control the party ratios of subcommittees, and these ratios generally reflect the party divisions in the chamber as a whole.[11]

On the basis of this study of party representation in conference, it would seem that, rather than discussing a tendency to overrepresent the minority party in conference, students of the legislature might more profitably be alerted to a tendency for party representation in conference to reflect the party distribution in the chamber as a whole. Clapp, Gross, and Steiner were probably correct in their assessment of overrepresentation on some conference committees, but generally the party representation on conference committees must be adjudged as reflecting the party divisions in the Senate and the House.

Differences between a Democratic and Republican Majority

Party representation on conference delegations reflects only one of many dimensions of party leadership in Congress. Party ratios in conference are determined by the chairman of the standing committee handling the bill to be discussed, and are not necessarily representative of the opinions of the formal party leadership in the Senate or House. Especially in the case of a Democrat-controlled Congress, a committee chairman may feel that Republican committee members are closer to his position on a particular bill than are members of his own party. In such a case, over-representation of the minority party in conference would not present the problems of opposition that would occur when an issue divided the membership along party lines.

We should expect party representation in conference to reflect the effectiveness and cohesion of the majority party. Thus, a cohesive majority party would be less likely to overrepresent the minority on conference committees than would a divided majority party. It must be recognized, however, that a large number of conference issues are not party issues. In such cases, party representation on the conference delegation is not a matter of great importance in the conference decision. During the period covered in this study, the proportion of roll calls on which a majority of the two parties took opposite stands has averaged under one-half of all roll calls.[12] Thus, many of the conferences included in our sample do not

11. George Goodwin, Jr., "Subcommittees: The Miniature Legislatures of Congress," *American Political Science Review,* LVI (September, 1962), 601.
12. Jewell and Patterson, *Legislative Process,* p. 419.

represent party issues, and therefore are conferences in which party representation on the delegation is a matter of little concern to the committee chairman.

Acknowledging the fact that party representation on conference committees is not as reliable an indicator of party leadership as are roll call votes, we would, nevertheless, expect party representation in conference to reflect differences between a Democratic and a Republican majority.

The five congresses studied include three Democratic congresses (the 79th, 88th, and 89th) and two Republican congresses (the 80th and 83d). In order to determine whether party representation in conference varied when the majority party varied, the distribution of party representation on conference committees for the two parties was calculated. Table 4

TABLE 4

REPRESENTATION OF MINORITY PARTY IN CONFERENCE IN DEMOCRATIC AND REPUBLICAN CONGRESSES

DEMOCRATIC CONGRESS (79th, 88th, and 89th; N = 357)		
Index of Representation *	House Delegation	Senate Delegation
Less than .9	21%	21%
.9 to .99	36	23
1.0 to 1.09	17	28
1.1 and over	26	28
REPUBLICAN CONGRESS (80th and 83d; N = 235)		
Less than .8	27%	36%
.8 to .89	32	49
.9 and over	41	15

* The index used here is the same used in Table 1, in which the conference percentage is compared to the percentage in the whole chamber.

shows the differences in representation for Democratic and Republican congresses.

It should be first noted that every conference during the Republican 80th and 83d congresses underrepresented the Democratic minority. In the second section of Table 4, the category .9 and over includes no conferences in which the Democrats were represented at the 1.0 level or above. This is in marked contrast to the 43% of the House conferences and the 56% of the Senate conferences in which the Republican minority was represented at the 1.0 level and above. Whether there is a Democratic or a Republican majority in Congress thus makes a great difference in party representation on conference.

Conference committees in a Democratic Congress tend to reflect the party divisions in the parent chamber. Fifty-three per cent of the House conference delegations and 51% of the Senate delegations reflected the Republican minority's strength in the chamber as a whole. A Democratic majority is also more likely to overrepresent the minority party in conference; all of the overrepresentative conferences included in this study occurred when the Democrats were in control of both houses. Thus, the observations of Clapp, Gross, and Steiner which revealed a tendency to overrepresent the minority party on conference are partially explained by the fact that their studies took place during periods of Democratic dominance.

To further test the differences between a Democratic and a Republican majority in terms of conference representation, a mean index of representation was computed for each chamber under Democratic and under Republican leadership. In the House, the mean index for Republican congresses is .86 while the mean for Democratic congresses is 1.01.[13] The Senate mean is .81 for the Republican congresses and 1.03 for Democratic congresses.[14] A difference-of-means test shows the differences in both houses to be significant at the .001 level.

In attempting to explain the differences in conference representation which occur in a Democratic or a Republican Congress, it is perhaps worthwhile to review some studies of the legislative party. Although none of these studies is directly concerned with party representation on conference committees, it is expected that conference representation is part of a more general pattern of party behavior which is reflected in the findings of roll call analyses.

In *The Congressional Party*, David Truman analyzes voting blocs in the 81st Congress in order to determine differences between the Democratic majority and the Republican minority. He found that, in both

13. For Democratic congresses, N = 357; for Republican, N = 235. A difference of means test produces Z = 4.89. The index used was that comparing conference representation with party representation in the whole house.

14. The samples for Democratic and Republican congresses are the same as in note 13; Z = 7.88.

houses, the minority party tended to be more fluid, with a voting structure which tended to shift more than did that of the majority. Using an index of cohesion, Truman also found that the Senate majority party was more cohesive than the minority, but in the House this pattern was reversed, the House minority party being slightly more cohesive than the majority.[15] During the period of the 81st Congress, the Democrats controlled both the Congress and the Presidency. Truman suggests that the latter is the more important factor in determining party cohesion in Congress, and in the case of divided government, the administration party, rather than the congressional majority party, would be the more cohesive.

Donald R. Matthews' study of the Senate during the period 1947 to 1957 again found that both Democrats and Republicans achieved their highest degree of party unity when their party also controlled the White House. Matthews notes, however, that "majority status in the Senate encourages party unity, even when the Presidency is controlled by the opposition party." [16] Over the ten-year period studied, the Senate Democrats were found to exhibit more party unity than Republicans. Acknowledging that the Senate party leaders were strengthened by party control of the White House, Matthews concludes that the Democratic leaders were more effective than the Republicans even when they were the opposition party.[17]

Matthews' findings are supported by Lee F. Anderson's study of the 80th, 83d, and 84th congresses. Using a scaling technique to measure the stability of party voting patterns, Anderson found that the majority had more stability, not only when it controlled the Presidency (the Republicans in the 83d Congress), but also when it was the opposition party (the Republicans in the 80th Congress and the Democrats in the 84th Congress).[18]

Malcolm Jewell and Samuel Patterson, in analyzing party unity in all congresses from 1949 to 1964, found that in the Senate the administration party had slightly higher cohesion than did the opposition party, whereas in the House there was no consistent difference in cohesion between administration and opposition parties.[19] Agreeing with the conclusions of Matthews and Anderson, they suggest that "a majority in Congress is at

15. Truman, *Congressional Party*, pp. 178, 281.
16. Matthews, *U.S. Senators*, p. 143.
17. *Ibid.*, p. 140.
18. Lee F. Anderson, "Variability in the Unidimensionality of Legislative Voting," *Journal of Politics*, XXVI (August, 1964), 568–85.
19. Jewell and Patterson, *Legislative Process*, p. 427.

least as important as control of the White House in producing greater party unity." [20]

The primary independent variables utilized in these studies have been those of majority or minority party and administration or opposition party. This study of party representation on conference committees does not permit full comparison with the earlier studies for two reasons. First, since the committee chairmen selecting conferees all come from the majority party, it is not possible to compare the majority and minority patterns of selecting conferees. Second, the congresses included in the sample represent three in which the congressional majority party and that of the administration were Democratic; one in which the majority party and that of the opposition were Republican; and one in which the majority party and the administration party were Republican. Because of the missing case of a Democratic majority in opposition, it would be impossible, here, to analyze conference representation in terms of the variables of majority administration and majority opposition party.

Analysis of the data does suggest that there is a marked difference between a Democratic majority and a Republican majority in terms of party representation in conference. If we consider overrepresentation of the minority party on conference committees to be an indicator of weak majority party leadership, the Republicans would seem to reflect more effective control as a majority party than do the Democrats. Realizing that such representation is controlled by the party's seniority leaders, rather than its elected floor leaders, and recognizing the predominance of southern Democrats in such seniority positions, the higher proportion of minority overrepresentation in Democratic congresses may be interpreted as reflecting a basic division within the Democratic party.

Again stressing the limits of comparability between party representation in conference and other indicators of party leadership, it is worth noting Jewell and Patterson's findings regarding party unity for the period 1949 to 1964. Although the differences are small, the Republican party scored slightly higher in party unity than did the Democrats throughout this period.[21] Jewell and Patterson did not, in this case, control for ideology as did Matthews, and one cannot therefore interpret party unity as a direct measure of the effectiveness of party leadership.

Table 4 indicates that there are differences between a Democratic and a Republican majority in terms of minority representation in conference.

20. *Ibid.*
21. *Ibid.*, p. 428.

In order to relate these differences to other research on congressional parties, one must recognize the limits of the measures involved and be explicit about the assumptions made. First, it is assumed that a cohesive majority party with effective leadership will tend to avoid overrepresentation of the minority party in conference. Second, it is assumed that the pattern of majority party unity in voting and the pattern of majority party control over conference representation are general reflections of the effectiveness of that party's leadership. Only then can it be noted that the findings of this study suggest that a Republican majority in Congress tends to provide more effective leadership than does a Democratic majority. Again it is emphasized that this is only a hypothesis indicated by an analysis of party representation in conference, and not a finding supported by adequate data. Future study, with more refined measures and a larger sample, would perhaps be a fruitful undertaking for students of the legislative process.

Any discussion of party representation in conference, and especially one which focuses on the representation, or overrepresentation, of the minority party, usually involves a hidden assumption. That assumption is that the two parties are divided over the issue in conference, and that overrepresentation of the minority party in conference can greatly hinder the majority party in obtaining a conference bill which reflects the majority opinion in that chamber. Gross seems to be referring to such a situation when he notes, "By joining with the opposition party, one dissident [majority party] member can swing the balance of power.[22] Steiner's reference to the "possible unsympathetic control at a crucial point in legislative action" reflects a similar concern.[23]

It should be recalled, therefore, that fewer than one-half of the conferences included in this study dealt with issues which divided Congress along party lines. Jefferson was quite precise about this distinction: "While it is usual to represent the party divisions of the House, the representation of opinions as to the pending differences is rather the more important consideration.[24] The question, then, is whether the pattern of selecting conferees, and especially the norm of seniority, often leads to an overrepresentation in conference of the minority opinion on the pending issue.

---

22. Gross, *Legislative Struggle,* p. 321.
23. Steiner, *Congressional Conference Committee,* p. 175.
24. Thomas Jefferson, *Jefferson's Manual* (Washington, D.C.: Government Printing Office, 1967), p. 260.

III

Seniority, Bill Support, and Conference Representation

That invariable following of the seniority rule can do great damage to the legislative process is clear beyond doubt. History is full of instances where incompetent or senile men have obstructed the national interest through their positions as committee chairmen attained through seniority.
—Senator Joseph Clark

Just because we are in Congress is no reason why we should not do practical things.
—Congressman Howard Smith

THE STANDARD of seniority evolved first in the Senate due to a reluctance to give its presiding officer, the Vice-President, the power of appointment. The Cannon Revolt of 1910 established the seniority system in the House, and today it is widely recognized as one of the more important variables affecting legislative behavior in Congress.[1] Samuel Hunt-

1. George Goodwin, Jr., "The Seniority System in Congress," *American Political Science Review*, LIII (June, 1959), 412–36. More recent studies include Michael Abram and Joseph Cooper, "The Rise of Seniority in the House of Representatives," *Polity*, I (Fall, 1968), 52–85; and Nelson Polsby, Miriam Gallaher, and Barry Rundquist, "The Growth of the Seniority System in the U.S. House of Representatives," *American Political Science Review*, LXIII (September, 1969), 787–807. Just as political scientists are beginning to understand all of the ramifications of seniority, the system seems likely to change. In October, 1970, House Republicans announced that ranking members would be chosen by a secret vote in the Republican Conference and that seniority would no longer be the sole criterion for selecting leaders. In December, a select nine-member committee appointed by the House Democratic caucus suggested a similar procedure for voting on committee chairmen.

ington notes that "only twice since the revolt of 1910, once in 1915 and once in 1921, has seniority been neglected in the choice of committee chairmen."[2]

The impact of the seniority norm is most evident in its use as the determining factor in selecting a committee chairman from the majority members of a committee. Not as obvious, however, is the influence of seniority in the initial choice of committee members. A brief outline of the procedures followed in appointing members to committee reveals the pervasive influence of seniority throughout the appointment process.

The House Democratic Committee on Committees is composed of the Democratic members of the Ways and Means Committee. The Ways and Means Committee is made up primarily of senior congressmen, and in the allocation of committee assignments the more senior members are extremely influential. Each member of the committee reviews applications for committee assignments from representatives in particular states. Requests for assignments are channeled to the committee through the senior Democrat of each state delegation.

The Republican Committee on Committees is composed of one member from each state with Republican representation. He is normally the senior member from that state. In both party committees it is the practice to consult senior members of the party on the committees where vacancies exist. These senior committee members have a virtual veto power on new members.[3]

The procedures for choosing committee members in the Senate are not as formal as those of the House. The Republican members of its Committee on Committees are nominated by the Republican Conference Chairman, subject to the approval of the Conference. Beginning in 1959, Republicans with the most seniority have permitted junior senators to have at least one seat on a major committee. When a conflict arises over a particular vacancy on a key committee, however, the Republicans have in most cases tended to follow the seniority rule.[4]

The Democratic Steering Committee, whose members are appointed by the floor leader and approved by the Democratic Conference, select mem-

2. Samuel P. Huntington, "Congressional Responses to the Twentieth Century," in *The Congress and America's Future*, ed. David B. Truman (Englewood Cliffs, N.J.: Prentice-Hall, 1965), p. 10.

3. Malcolm Jewell and Samuel Patterson, *The Legislative Process in the United States*, 2d ed. (New York: Random House, 1966), p. 214. See also Nicholas A. Masters, "Committee Assignments," in *New Perspectives on the House of Representatives*, ed. Robert L. Peabody and Nelson Polsby (Chicago: Rand McNally, 1963), pp. 33–58.

4. *Ibid.*, p. 215.

bers for vacant positions. The famous Johnson Rule of 1953 permitted departures from seniority in making appointments by refusing a second top committee assignment to senior Democrats until every party member had one such assignment.[5]

These procedures for making initial committee assignments indicate that seniority is an important factor affecting the distribution of influence within Congress. Though not as automatically and inflexibly applied as in the determination of committee chairmen, the norm of seniority in initial committee assignments and transfers has an obvious impact on factors affecting legislative output. Charles Clapp remarks on the differences between the two parties and the two houses in this respect:

> The importance of seniority in making committee assignments varies from party to party and from one house to the other. It is followed most closely by Senate Republicans and least closely by Senate Democrats, with the House groups falling somewhere between them.[6]

Many students of legislative behavior, having observed the impact of the Johnson Rule and the Republicans' later adoption of a similar procedure, have noted that seniority seems to have declined in importance as a major factor in committee assignments. A case often cited to illustrate this is the appointment, in 1957, of Senator John Kennedy over the more senior Senator Estes Kefauver to a coveted position on the Foreign Relations Committee.[7] The way in which seniority was circumvented in this instance is perhaps more instructive of the importance of seniority in committee assignments than is the simple fact that it did not determine the outcome:

> After the presidential election of 1956, Estes Kefauver of Tennessee and John F. Kennedy of Massachusetts, who had competed on the National Convention floor at Chicago for the vice presidential nomination the previous summer, were competing again, this time for a single vacancy on Foreign Relations.
>
> Johnson, who had backed Kennedy against Kefauver at Chicago, was now trying to bring Kennedy closer to his orbit. He was determined to

---

5. Goodwin, "Seniority System," p. 416; and Donald R. Matthews, *U.S. Senators and Their World* (New York: Random House, Vintage Books, 1960), p. 128.

6. Charles L. Clapp, *The Congressman: His Work as He Sees It* (New York: Doubleday, Anchor Books, 1964), p. 227 n.

7. For example, see Marian Irish and James Prothro, *The Politics of American Democracy* (Englewood Cliffs, N.J.: Prentice-Hall, 1965), p. 315.

have the vacancy go to Kennedy over Johnson's old foe, Kefauver. But how to get around Kefauver's four year seniority bulge over Kennedy? In December, 1956, long before Congress convened, Johnson telephoned Anderson with a most curious question: "How are you getting along with your campaign for the Foreign Relations Committee?"

Anderson was puzzled. Could Johnson have forgotten that his "campaign" had ended two years earlier? But Johnson persisted.

"This may be your chance," he said.

Before Anderson could reply that he had his hands full as chairman of Atomic Energy, Johnson rushed on.

"You have seniority now over Jack Kennedy," Johnson explained. "But if you don't claim it, Estes Kefauver may get there first."

Johnson's ploy suddenly came through to Anderson. Both Anderson and Kefauver were members of the Class of '48, and therefore had equal seniority. If they both applied for one vacancy on the Foreign Relations Committee, Johnson could throw up his hands in the Steering Committe, declare a standoff, and give the vacancy to Kennedy. Anderson went along with this neat strategy, and Kennedy was given the seat.[8]

As the Kennedy-Kefauver conflict of 1957 illustrates, the norm of seniority in committee assignments is still an important factor in determining who gets on the committee and how. Though more flexible than it was prior to 1953, it still greatly influences who is going to select new committee members, and who is going to be selected for the more attractive vacancies. The Kennedy appointment shows not only the flexibility of the system, but also the necessity of working within the system to harvest the fruits of that flexibility.

Seniority and Subcommittees

The Legislative Reorganization Act of 1941, by reducing the number of standing committees from eighty-one to thirty-four, led to the proliferation of subcommittees in both houses. Recent congresses have included over two hundred subcommittees.[9] George Goodwin has observed that the subcommittee system gives a great deal of flexibility to the seniority system by allowing less senior committee members to play

---

8. Rowland Evans and Robert Novak, *Lyndon B. Johnson: The Exercise of Power* (New York: New American Library, 1966), p. 101.

9. For the effects of this proliferation of subcommittees, see Huntington, "Congressional Responses," p. 20.

effective legislative roles.[10] A freshman Republican in the House confirms Goodwin's observation:

> There isn't any bigger myth than the idea that new people can't do anything. After all this talk about seniority, I was surprised. You know you aren't going to be the committee chairman, and you know you aren't going to get to sponsor a major piece of legislation, but other than that you can participate as much as you want.
>
> You even get to take leadership on a bill in committee. Every time a bill comes out, the young members are asked to take five minutes or ten minutes to speak on the floor. They ask us; we don't have to ask. So it's just the opposite from what the myth and fiction of seniority would have you believe.[11]

The congressman speaking was a member of the House Education and Labor Committee. Richard Fenno points out that on this particular committee, "The weakness of seniority traditions is also evident in the fact that very senior members are sometimes denied the sponsorship of a bill or the chairmanship of a subcommittee to which their rank would otherwise entitle them." [12] The importance of seniority in distributing the work load of the committee varies greatly from committee to committee, as does the importance of subcommittees in handling legislative work.

Some committees, such as the Senate Finance Committee and the House Ways and Means Committee, have no subcommittees even though they deal with such diverse topics as taxes and reciprocal trade. In both the House and Senate Appropriations committees, however, the subcommittees handle the bulk of the work. Charles Clapp estimates that about one-half of the legislation coming out of the House Armed Services Committee passes through the full committee route, and notes that the Foreign Affairs Committee, although it has ten subcommittees, considers its major legislation in the full committee.[13] In some committees, such as Education and Labor, the chairman may bypass senior members of the

---

10. George Goodwin, Jr., "Subcommittees: The Miniature Legislatures of Congress," *American Political Science Review*, LVI (September, 1962), 596–604; and Goodwin, *The Little Legislatures: Committees of Congress* (Amherst: University of Massachusetts Press, 1970), pp. 45–63.

11. Quoted in Richard F. Fenno, "The House of Representatives and Federal Aid to Education," in *New Perspectives on the House of Representatives*, ed. Robert L. Peabody and Nelson Polsby (Chicago: Rand McNally, 1963), pp. 206–7.

12. *Ibid.*, p. 207.

13. Clapp, *The Congressman*, p. 269. For an excellent recent discussion of this variety in committee-subcommittee relations, see Goodwin, *The Little Legislatures*, pp. 45–63.

committee by denying them chairmanship of a subcommittee or by establishing a system of subcommittees lacking in specified areas of permanent jurisdiction.[14] In other committees, seniority greatly influences the distribution of subcommittee chairmanships and committee work. A Republican member of the Senate Appropriations Committee explained the procedure there to Richard Fenno:

> At the beginning of each year we hold a meeting, and we go down the line by seniority. Styles Bridges has the most seniority and he says he wants to be ranking member of some subcommittee—I've forgotten what. Then Leverett Saltonstall, and he takes Armed Services and so on. Then we go down the line again and say which subcommittee we want to be on next.[15]

A study of the impact of seniority on subcommittees reveals that there is great variation from committee to committee. As in the case of committee assignments, the norm of seniority greatly affects the distribution of influence, but it is not a completely inflexible system. There are many instances where chairmen, working within the general rules of seniority, have been able to deny influence over committee legislation to a senior member of the committee. Jewell and Patterson provide us with a general statement about seniority and subcommittees:

> A further effect of the seniority rule is that most subcommittee chairmen are senior members of the committees. On about two-thirds of the committees there are no exceptions to this rule, and on the rest there are only a few examples of congressmen being bypassed to give subcommittee chairmanships to junior members.
>
> Rarely does a committee chairman ignore seniority because of policy considerations in making subcommittee assignments. Moreover, the chairmen of subcommittees are likely to hold these positions with as much tenacity as committee chairmen do.[16]

14. An example is Chairman Adam Clayton Powell's establishing a General Education Subcommittee, a Select Education Subcommittee, and a Special Education Subcommittee. He offered the chairmanship of the Special Education Subcommittee to the senior congressman, Landrum of Georgia. Landrum, sensing that he might have a subcommittee with no legislation, declined. Richard Fenno, "House of Representatives," p. 207. Powell's offering the chairmanship illustrates again that flexibility in the seniority system is exercised within the general limits established by the system itself.

15. Richard Fenno, *The Power of the Purse: Appropriations Politics in Congress* (Boston: Little, Brown, 1966), p. 544.

16. Jewell and Patterson, *Legislative Process*, p. 219.

The influence of seniority on the committee and subcommittee structure in Congress is seen as being a major factor at many different points in the system. Senior members exercise great control over initial committee assignments and transfers. Committee seniority automatically determines who will be the committee chairman. The membership and chairmanships of subcommittees are generally allocated by the committee chairman in terms of seniority. As we have seen, however, the seniority system is not an inviolable one. There are means of exercising leadership within the general rules of seniority in such a way as to greatly alter its effects on the structure of Congress. As one member of Congress has noted:

> Seniority may control if all other things are equal. But other things usually are not equal. Sometimes you begin to think seniority is little more than a device to fall back on when it is convenient to do so.[17]

Seniority and Conference Representation

Just as seniority generally determines who will be on which committees, and membership and seniority determine who will be on which subcommittees, so also do membership and seniority on the committee and subcommittee determine who will be on the conference committee. The seniority standard both directly and indirectly influences the selection of conferees. "The conference committee," said Congressman Clem Miller, "is the ultimate flowering of the power of seniority." [18]

Reliance on seniority in the selection of conferees is a long-standing practice in both houses. Ada McCown, one of the earliest students of the conference committee, comments on the development of this practice:

> The modern practice in both houses has been to choose as the majority members of the conference committee the chairman and the majority member second in seniority on the committee reporting the bill and having it in charge, and as the minority member of the conference committee, the ranking minority member of the committee having the bill in charge.

17. Quoted in Clapp, *The Congressman*, p. 226.
18. John W. Baker, ed., *Member of the House: Letters of a Congressman* (New York: Scribner's, 1962), p. 114.

When there has been a larger number on the conference committee, the additional members have been chosen according to position on the same committee. This custom developed gradually and did not become general until late in the nineteenth century.

There was opposed to it a belief that the conference chairman should reflect the opinion of the body which it represented, that is, the opinion of that body on the particular bill to be considered. This could not be so in every case if the principle was always followed. In the end, for different reasons, partly through efforts at reform, the principle of seniority has prevailed.[19]

The impact of seniority on the selection of conferees is not simply the direct effect of this norm on the conference selection process, but rather the cumulative effects of seniority in determining committee and subcommittee position as well as conference representation. The results of such cumulative patterns of influence are described by Daniel Berman:

> This system of appointing conferees makes it highly unlikely that a junior member of Congress will ever represent his house at the time when legislation is being put into final form.
>
> Senator Proxmire of Wisconsin discovered that only 26 of 64 Democrats in the Senate were serving on conference committees on a particular day which he studied. Many of the select few were participating in several conferences at the same time, although 38 Democratic senators had no assignments at all.[20]

Flexibility in the Seniority Systems

It should be noted, however, that there is not one seniority system operating in Congress, but three. The first is seniority in the chamber: the uninterrupted period of time that a representative or senator has served in that body. This system influences the organization of Congress primarily through initial committee assignments, committee transfers, and the election of formal leaders.[21]

19. Ada C. McCown, *The Congressional Conference Committee* (New York: Columbia University Press, 1927), p. 149.

20. Daniel M. Berman, *In Congress Assembled: The Legislative Process in the National Government,* 2d ed. (New York: Macmillan, 1966), p. 306.

21. Seniority, by itself, does not determine party leadership. In many cases, a relatively junior member will be elevated to a leadership position (e.g., Johnson became Senate Minority Leader after serving only four years). In the case of Speaker of the House, the

The second system bases seniority on length of service on a particular standing committee. It is committee seniority which determines the chairman and ranking member. Because of the patterns of committee transfers, a junior member in terms of house seniority may rank above his fellow members in terms of committee seniority. He will be the chairman or ranking minority member because of his committee seniority.

The third system of seniority is that of subcommittee seniority. Varying greatly from committee to committee, the influence of subcommittee seniority is most obvious in the case of standing committees which have had permanent subcommittees over a long period of time. The impact of subcommittee seniority on the structure of Congress is most evident in the appointment of a conference committee. In 1950, Gilbert Steiner remarked:

> A tradition has not yet developed as to whether subcommittee members deserve a preferred place on the conference committee over ranking members of the full committee originally involved.
> Indeed, the seniority principle itself has sometimes been ignored, and this has led to charges of "packing" the conference with proponents of a point of view supported by the standing committee chairman and the presiding officer of the house involved.[22]

It was noted earlier that the seniority systems determining committee membership and subcommittee chairmanships were ones which, because of their flexibility, allowed legislative leaders to exercise a control over the organization of Congress which the seniority system, at first glance, seemed to deny. Steiner's observation indicates that there is the same sort of flexibility in the seniority system which determines who will sit in conference. The rule suggests that conferees be the members of the committee involved with the legislation who have the most seniority. It does not, however, specify whether these are to be the senior members of the full committee or the senior members of the subcommittee. In some cases, conference representation following committee seniority would produce a conference delegation quite different from one following subcommittee seniority. This does occur in the House Appropriations Committee.

---

influence of seniority is more obvious. Speaker McCormack had served thirty-four years at the time of his selection as Speaker. For a discussion of this trend, see Nelson M. Polsby, "The Institutionalization of the U.S. House of Representatives," *American Political Science Review*, LXII (March, 1968), 144–68.

22. Gilbert Y. Steiner, *The Congressional Conference Committee: Seventieth to Eightieth Congresses* (Urbana: University of Illinois Press, 1950), p. 8.

The committee chairman, by having the option of following committee or subcommittee seniority in appointing managers, is able to exercise a control over conference representation which would be precluded by a single seniority system. Here again, we find that the leadership of Congress is able to exercise flexibility within the general framework of the seniority system itself.

In order to determine patterns of seniority in conference, the standing committee seniority rank and, when applicable, the subcommittee seniority rank of each conferee included in this study were obtained from *The Congressional Quarterly*. Each conference delegation was then investigated to see whether the appointment of conferees more closely followed committee or subcommittee seniority. The results of this study are shown in Table 5.

TABLE 5

PERCENTAGE OF CONFERENCE APPOINTMENTS FOLLOWING SENIORITY SYSTEMS

	House (N = 460) *	Senate (N = 460)	House and Senate (N = 920)
Committee seniority	32%	37%	35%
Subcommittee seniority	49	46	47
Committee and subcommittee seniority equal	1	3	2
Neither committee nor subcommittee seniority **	18	14	16

* The N for each house drops to 460 here because the 136 conferences in the 79th Congress were dropped from this part of the study. Since the 79th Congress predates the Congressional Reorganization Act 1946, subcommittees played little or no role in the processing of these conference bills.
** To be included in the "neither" category, a conference delegation was required to have excluded two senior members in both parties from both the committee and the subcommittee; or, in cases where there were no subcommittees involved in the handling of the bill, to have excluded two senior members in both parties from the standing committee.

The most striking feature of Table 5 is the similarity between the House and Senate patterns of following seniority in appointing conferees. In both houses a greater number of conference delegations followed subcommittee, rather than standing committee, seniority. The fact that this pattern prevailed in both the House and the Senate contrasts with Jewell and Patterson's conclusion that "there seems to be a greater tendency in the Senate than in the House to use the senior members, and occasionally all members, of subcommittees on conference committees.[23] This study suggests that it is more correct to speak of a tendency to use the senior members of the subcommittee on conference delegations in both the House and the Senate.

A rather surprising finding was the number of conferences to which conferees were appointed in seeming violation of the seniority norm; 16 per cent of the total conference delegations studied reflected deviation from both committee and subcommittee seniority, with the House having slightly more cases than the Senate.[24]

Although Table 5 represents general patterns of seniority in conference delegations, it tends to greatly underemphasize the following of subcommittee seniority in appointing conferees. This results from the fact that not all bills which go to conference pass through the subcommittee stage. Because of either the nature of the bill or the committee handling it, the bill is often considered only in the full committee. Of the total of 460 conference bills in each chamber, 206 in the House and 216 in the Senate were never processed through a subcommittee. Table 6

TABLE 6

Percentage of Conference Appointments Involving a Subcommittee Only Following Seniority Systems

	House (N = 254)	Senate (N = 244)	House and Senate (N = 498)
Committee seniority	11%	13%	12%
Subcommittee seniority	89	87	88

indicates the patterns of committee/subcommittee seniority in conference representation which emerge when we control for bills not handled by a subcommittee.

We find that the slight tendency to follow subcommittee seniority noted earlier becomes much more pronounced when we eliminate those cases in which there was no subcommittee handling the bill. Table 6

23. Jewell and Patterson, *Legislative Process,* p. 476.

24. Illness, absence from Washington, or an expressed wish not to serve in conference will often result in the absence of certain senior members from conference committees. To allow for such instances, conferences were classified as following "neither seniority systems" only when two senior members from each party were skipped in the appointment of conferees. See the note to Table 5.

suggests that we may confidently speak of a tendency to follow subcommittee seniority in the appointment of conferees.

Again we notice that Jewell and Patterson's discussion of a greater proclivity to follow subcommittee seniority on the part of Senate chairmen is not borne out by these findings. The two houses are remarkably similar in their tendency to follow subcommittee seniority in appointing managers.

A general consideration of the patterns of seniority in conference representation suggests that there does exist a norm of seniority in appointing conferees. For those bills which have been processed through a subcommittee, the norm is one of the following subcommittee, rather than standing committee, seniority in appointing conferees.

This norm of following subcommittee seniority, coupled with the fact that almost one-half of the bills studied involved no subcommittee action, suggests that the options of the chairman in appointing conferees are more restricted than was initially supposed. In cases involving no subcommittee, the chairman is not provided with a choice between two seniority systems. In cases which do involve subcommittee action, there exists a norm of following subcommittee seniority in appointing conferees.

That flexibility within the seniority system exists is evidenced by the number of cases which ignored both committee and subcommittee seniority and by the number of cases which followed committee seniority even though a subcommittee was involved in processing the conference bill. That this flexibility is not as great as was initially conjectured is indicated by the large number of conference bills involving no subcommittee and by the existence of a norm of following subcommittee seniority when applicable.

Seniority and Democratic and Republican Majorities

As was noted earlier, Charles Clapp found that the importance of seniority in making committee assignments varied from party to party and chamber to chamber. In order to determine whether there exists a pattern similar to that observed by Clapp in appointing conferees, seniority in conference was studied in terms of party control of the Congress.

Table 7 reveals that there are no great differences between Democratic and Republican chairmen following seniority in appointing conferees. If the phenomenon discussed by Clapp extended to the appointment of conferees, we would expect Senate delegations in a Democratic Congress to display the greatest deviation from seniority. We find, however, that Democratic Senate delegations had the lowest percentage of conferences which completely deviated from seniority. In contrast to the 8 per cent of Democratic Senate delegations which followed neither committee nor subcommittee seniority, we find that 20 per cent of the Republican Senate delegations deviated from seniority. The differences are small, but the direction of variation is the opposite of what might be expected on the basis of generalizing Clapp's statement regarding seniority norms within the two parties.

One hesitates to draw inferences from the pattern of variation represented in Table 7 because of the small differences involved. The tendency to follow subcommittee seniority in appointing conferees seems to extend across both houses and both parties. In order to get a clearer picture of this tendency, the findings in Table 8 again limit consideration to only those conference bills which went through subcommittee.

These findings, while indicating again the tendency to follow subcommittee seniority in conference appointment, suggest that the two parties differ in their adherence to this norm. Democratic chairmen tend to follow subcommittee seniority in conference more closely than do Republican chairmen.[25]

The Democratic tendency to rely on subcommittee seniority could possibly reflect the longer tenure of the Democrats as the majority party. The longer a party exercises control over the structure of Congress, the more likely there is to be specification of function within the legislature. Such specification would be reflected in a greater reliance on subcommittees in the legislative process. At the conference stage, this would result in the chamber's managers being selected from the subcommittee rather than from the standing committee.

A party which had not been the majority in Congress over a long period of time, such as the Republicans in the 80th and 83d congresses, would be less likely to have developed a pattern of specification and a reliance on subcommittees. The selection of conferees would thus tend to focus more on the standing committee handling the legislation.

25. Because the Democratic congresses studied were more recent than the Republican congresses, it was hypothesized that this difference in following subcommittee seniority might be more a function of an increased reliance on subcommittees in recent congresses than of party differences. A study of this trend in each separate Congress, however, revealed that reliance on subcommittee seniority was not linear over time, and suggested that the differences were more a function of party control of Congress.

TABLE 7

Percentage of Conference Appointments Following Seniority Systems by Majority Party

	Democratic Majority			Republican Majority		
	House (N = 223)	Senate (N = 223)	House and Senate (N = 446)	House (N = 237)	Senate (N = 237)	House and Senate (N = 474)
Committee seniority	32%	37%	35%	33%	37%	35%
Subcommittee seniority	51	52	51	47	41	44
Committee and subcommittee seniority equal	0	3	2	1	2	1
Neither committee nor sub-committee seniority	17	8	12	19	20	20

TABLE 8

Percentage of Conference Appointments Involving a Subcommittee Only Following Seniority Systems by Majority Party

	Democratic Majority			Republican Majority		
	House (N = 122)	Senate (N = 126)	House and Senate (N = 248)	House (N = 132)	Senate (N = 118)	House and Senate (N = 250)
Committee seniority	7%	9%	8%	16%	17%	16%
Subcommittee seniority	93	91	92	84	83	84

The rather limited findings of this study do not provide a solid basis for generalizations about the influence of party differences on the seniority system. We have found that seniority seems to be less important in determining conference representation when the Republicans control the Senate. Democratic chairmen in both houses demonstrated a more pronounced tendency to follow subcommittee seniority than did Republican chairmen. However, if we are to make general statements about the influence of seniority on conference representation, the variable of party control of Congress must be relegated to a relatively minor position, for, in both parties and in both houses, we have found a general tendency to follow subcommittee seniority in appointing conferees.

Representation of Minority Opinion

As in the case of party representation in conference, we are not so much concerned with the simple existence of seniority in appointing conferees as we are interested in determining the effects of such a pattern of representation. Many observers have commented on the effects of following seniority in appointing conferees. That there is some agreement as to these effects is indicated by the comments of Jewell and Patterson:

> The reliance on seniority in the choice of members makes it possible, however, that a majority of the senators or representatives on the committee will be men who voted against the bill or, more likely, who voted against the majority in their house on one of the amendments that is in dispute between the two houses.[26]

The most obvious result of this reliance on seniority in appointing conferees is seen to be that conferees who have opposed the bill in their chamber are unlikely to be strong advocates of that chamber's view in the conference bargaining. Senator Eugene McCarthy, referring to a conference session which lasted less than half an hour, suggested a means of reducing congressional embarrassment in these situations:

> At least, when we go to conference, we ought to walk slowly on the way . . . and very slowly on the way back, so at least one hour would elapse from the time we sent conferees to negotiate for a settlement and

---

26. Jewell and Patterson, *Legislative Process*, p. 476. Also see Berman, *In Congress Assembled*, pp. 306 ff., and Clapp, *The Congressman*, p. 278.

the time they came back to the Senate to tell us that they could not do anything against the firm stand of the House of Representatives.[27]

The rapid surrender of one house to the other is only one of many possible effects of the use of the seniority norm in appointing conference delegations. Bertram Gross suggests that:

> If one wanted to stretch the point a little, one might whimsically claim that any similarity between the views of the House or the Senate and those of the conferees representing the House or the Senate is purely coincidental. Many members come to a conference committee eager to defend the views represented in the bill passed by the other house or to strike out provisions inserted in their own house.[28]

Such a case occurred in the 1967 conference on the congressional redistricting bill when Senator Sam J. Ervin, Jr., argued for the House version and Congressman Emanuel Celler argued for the Senate version. The confused conference committee eventually abandoned any hope of a compromise.

The redistricting conference certainly is not representative of most conferences. But situations in which the seniority system has resulted in the appointment of conferees opposed to their chamber's position occur frequently enough to be a recurring object of congressional reform. Perhaps the chief advocate of reform in this area is ex-Senator Joseph Clark. The former Democratic senator from Pennsylvania has long advocated an amendment to the Senate rules "which would require that the Senate members of the conference committee should be chosen from those who have indicated, by their votes, their concurrence with the prevailing view of the Senate on matters in disagreement with the House."[29]

How often seniority leads to conference situations of the type Senator Clark seeks to correct is a matter of speculation. A 1959 study conducted by *The Congressional Quarterly* found only four conferences exhibiting these characteristics.[30]

It also should be noted that the effects of seniority on conference representation are not all biased in the same direction. Although Senator Clark and most political scientists who comment on the subject tend to focus

27. Senate, *Congressional Record*, 87th Cong., 2d sess., 1962, 108, pt. 4, A–2490; quoted in Berman, *In Congress Assembled*, p. 307.

28. Bertram Gross, *The Legislative Struggle* (New York: McGraw-Hill, 1953), p. 321.

29. Senate, *Congressional Record*, 88th Cong., 2d sess., 1964, 110, pt. 17, 22584.

30. *Congressional Quarterly Weekly Report*, XVII, no. 18, 1959, 597–98.

on cases where the effect of seniority is to give conference representation to members who oppose their chamber's bill, the seniority system can produce another effect, i.e., when all of the senior members on the conference delegation supported the legislation which passed, while junior members of the committee or subcommittee, not on the conference delegation, opposed the legislation. In such a case, the "representation of opinions as to the pending legislation" outlined in *Jefferson's Manual* would not take place.

We thus find Senator Wayne Morse attacking the principle of seniority in conference for reasons in contradistinction to those which were advanced by Senator Clark:

> I am very unhappy about the selection of the conferees for the conference on the foreign aid bill. It was very interesting where the line was drawn this year in the selection of conferees, a selection based on the unexcusable principle of seniority that prevails in the Senate.
>
> The line was carefully drawn, in selecting the conferees for the conference on the foreign aid bill, at a point where not a single Senator opposed to the bill was selected. That is an interesting commentary, because when we find that kind of stacked procedure, we cannot expect the conference to have had presented to it very effectively the point of view of the opposition.[31]

The differences between Senator Clark's and Senator Morse's positions on conference representation seem to reflect a more general disagreement over representational roles. One school, represented here by Clark, contends that the conference representative should support the constituency's policy decision, which is the position of a majority of the constituency. In conference terms, this means that a Senate manager should support the position taken by the majority in his chamber. The Morse position, however, is one which favors representation of the constituency policy debate rather than policy decision. This means that the conflicts existing in the constituency should be brought into the representative body which is making the policy decision. Thus a conference delegation should represent both majority and minority opinion in the parent chamber.

In this chapter we are primarily concerned with the often observed tendency for seniority to produce a conference delegation composed of members who do not support their chamber's decision on the conference bill. In order to determine how often this occurs, votes of all committee,

---

31. Senate, *Congressional Record*, 88th Cong., 1st sess., 1963, 109, pt. 18, 24434.

subcommitee, and conference members were studied for those conference bills involving a roll call vote. The actual percentage of supporters of the bill in conference was then computed for each case and was contrasted with the percentage of supporters which would have obtained had strict committee seniority and strict subcommittee seniority been followed in the appointment of conferees. In the overwhelming majority of conferences, it was found that there was no difference between the actual percentage of conferees supporting their chamber's position and that which would have obtained had seniority been strictly followed in appointing conferees.[32]

The focus of the study was then narrowed to a consideration of only those conferences in which there was a difference between actual supporter representation and that which the following of seniority would have produced. To arrive at a general understanding of this pattern, the mean per cent of supporters on conference committees was computed for all such conferences, and for the hypothetical cases of following committee and subcommittee seniority (Fig. 1).

A difference-of-means test was applied to both of the differences presented in Figure 1 and, in the case of deviation from committee seniority, the difference was found to be statistically significant.[33] The fact that the difference of means in the subcommittee samples was not significant, coupled with the fact that the mean per cent of supporters in conference obtained by following subcommittee seniority was the same as the increased mean per cent of supporters obtained by deviating from committee seniority, suggests that reliance on subcommittee rather than full committee seniority in appointing conferees tends to increase the number of supporters of a bill on conference committees.

We found earlier that there seemed to be a norm of following subcommittee seniority in appointing conferees. The findings here suggest that one effect of this norm is to increase the representation in conference of members who support their chamber's position on the conference bill.

Parts *a* and *b* of Figure 1 are perhaps even more instructive in their indication that, when a difference exists in the number of supporters gained by following committee seniority in appointing conferees and the number

32. In 128 of the 191 conferences with a roll call studied in terms of committee seniority, there was no difference between the proportion of supporters actually obtained and that which would have obtained had strict committee seniority been followed; 74 of the 86 conferences studied in terms of subcommittee seniority showed the same pattern.

33. For the committee difference of .12, $Z = 1.51$, $p = .06$; for the subcommittee difference of .6, $Z = .38$, $p = .35$.

FIGURE 1. Seniority and the Representation of Bill Supporters in
Conference

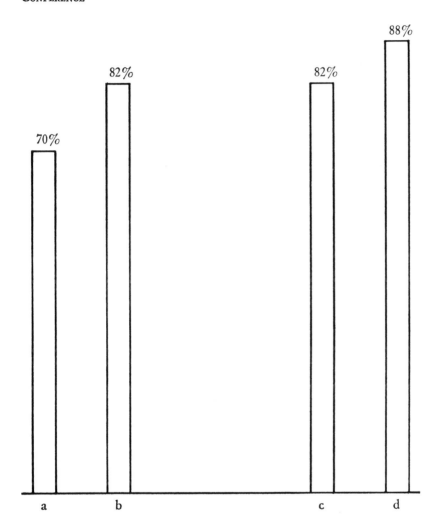

a. Mean per cent supporters on conference committee, following seniority
(N = 63).
b. Actual mean per cent supporters on conference committee (no subcommittee involved; N = 63).
c. Mean per cent supporters on conference committee, following subcommittee seniority (N = 12).
d. Actual mean per cent supporters on conference committee (subcommittee involved; N = 12).

of supporters gained by deviating from seniority, there is a tendency for the chairman to deviate from seniority and to increase the representation of supporters on the conference delegation. If committee seniority had been followed in the conferences studied, the mean per cent of supporters in conference would have been 70. By deviating from seniority the appointing chairmen increased this mean per cent to 82.

Again, we become aware of the flexibility in the seniority system as it affects conference representation. By often having the option of following subcommittee or committee seniority, the chairman is able to exercise control over conference representation. The general pattern seems to be one of following subcommittee seniority, and this has the effect of increasing the proportion of the conference delegation supporting its chamber's position.

But even when the chairman does not have this option of following committee or subcommittee seniority, he is able to exercise control over conference representation by not appointing some senior members who opposed the bill in that house.

Many conferences no doubt reflect the influence of seniority on conference representation which Senator Clark sought to correct. If we seek, however, to determine general patterns relating seniority, support of the bill, and conference representation, we must be aware of the effects of the dual seniority system and the general flexibility which this system exhibits.

The emphasis, throughout this chapter, on the flexibility of the seniority system was motivated by Lewis Froman's observation:

> Very few people are against the seniority system entirely. The major advantage of the seniority system is that it distributes power within the party and within the House and Senate automatically.
> This is perceived by most people, as being very advantageous. It avoids the inevitable fights which would occur if the seniority system were not part of the procedure.
> What people are against, however, is the inflexibility of the seniority system.[34]

The findings of this study indicate that the seniority norm is not of such rigidity as to preclude the exercise of leadership options. It does not automatically lead to conference delegations opposed to their own chamber's bill. It allows the members and the leadership to do "practical things."

34. Lewis A. Froman, Jr., *The Congressional Process* (Boston: Little, Brown, 1967), p. 178.

IV

The Conference Decision:
Patterns of One-House
Dominance

When the House and Senate come to a sharp difference of opinion upon any subject of legislation which really interests the people, the advantage is sometimes with the one, sometimes with the other. The Senate has the advantage of being a public council, not a mere congeries of committees, and of setting forth its reasons in thorough debate.

The House has the advantage of being regarded as the more truly representative chamber and of being more directly in touch with the general sentiment of the country. The House also has the advantage of being under thorough discipline and standing ready to do what it is told to do promptly when it becomes necessary to maneuver for position in such a contest of wills.

But what happens at last is proof of nothing, however the contest may end. It does not prove the popular sympathy of the House, if it win, nor the better counsel of the Senate, if it win.

—Woodrow Wilson

IN THE two preceding chapters, our theoretical framework has focused on two systems, the House and the Senate. We have analyzed the output of representation on the conference delegations primarily in terms of the interactions within each of these systems. In this chapter, the conference committee itself is conceived as a system, and our focus shifts to policy output as represented by the conference decision. It should be emphasized that the interdependence among the various elements of these systems is very great, but an analytical distinction is useful in terms of organizing this study. An output of the conference committee system enters the House and Senate systems as an input which greatly affects future conference delegation outputs.

The conference decision outputs will be studied here, not in terms of the larger political system, but rather in terms of the interrelationship of the House and Senate systems. Measurement of these outputs is thus undertaken, not along such dimensions as government expenditures, liberalism-conservatism, or centralization-decentralization, but rather in terms of relative House and Senate influence in the conference system. "The central question of conference committee decision making is, 'Who wins?'" writes Richard Fenno. "It must be answered before the other important questions of 'how' and 'why' can be broached."[1]

Gilbert Steiner's comprehensive study of fifty-six conferences distributed over ten policy areas in the 70th to 80th congresses sought to determine general patterns of relative House and Senate influence in conference. Steiner found that the influence of the House of Representatives far outweighed that of the Senate in determining conference outcomes. In thirty-two instances (57%) the House conference delegation was found to be more influential than that of the Senate. Senate predominance obtained in fifteen (27%) of the conferences studied, and nine (16%) of the conferences were adjudged as being an even split between the positions of the two chambers. Summarizing these findings, Steiner suggests that the House generally prevails in conference, except perhaps in the area of fiscal policy.[2]

If we accept Steiner's generalization of House superiority in conference as being correct, we may look to the structural differences between the two chambers in seeking to explain this pattern. The House, although it has over four times as many members as the Senate, has only four more committees. This results in a senator's sitting on three to five committees as compared to the representative's one to two. The effect of this difference between the two chambers is seen mainly in the greater degree

1. Richard F. Fenno, *The Power of the Purse: Appropriations Politics in Congress* (Boston: Little, Brown, 1966), p. 661. See also Jeffrey L. Pressman, *House vs. Senate: Conflict in the Appropriations Process* (New Haven: Yale University Press, 1966), pp. 62–63.

2. Gilbert Y. Steiner, *The Congressional Conference Committee: Seventieth to Eightieth Congresses* (Urbana: University of Illinois Press, 1950), pp. 170–72.

of subject matter specialization in the House as compared to that in the Senate. "It does seem clear," observe Jewell and Patterson, "that House members, to be maximally effective, are required, more than Senators, to develop expertise in a single subject matter specialty." [3]

Generally speaking, then, we would expect House conferees to be more familiar with specific aspects of legislation in conference than their Senate counterparts. Richard Fenno says of the appropriations conferences:

> By general agreement, the House conferees are better prepared, better organized, better informed, more single-minded in their interest, and employ a more belligerent bargaining style. . . . Because the House seems to possess so many resources, it may have come as quite a surprise to find all the data indicating that it loses more often than it wins.[4]

In his study of 288 appropriations conferences in which one or the other house prevailed, Fenno discovered the Senate winning 65% of these conferences, and the House, 35%.[5]

Recognizing the discrepancies between the findings of Steiner and Fenno, we can still try to determine if it is possible to make general statements about patterns of one-house dominance. Steiner's study focuses on conferences between 1928 and 1948. Only five appropriations conferences are included in his sample (one in 1928, two in 1929, one in 1933, and one in 1943). Fenno's sample consists of 331 appropriations conferences occurring between 1947 and 1962.

3. Malcolm Jewell and Samuel Patterson, *The Legislative Process in the United States,* 2d ed. (New York: Random House, 1966), p. 369. This greater specialization in the House is also reflected in Paletz's finding that 50% of the senators participated in six or more conferences, whereas the comparable figures for the House ranged from a low of 4.6% to a high of 14.25% (based on conference participation for the 86th through the 90th congresses). See David Paletz, "Influence in Congress: An Analysis of the Nature and Effects of Conference Committees" (Paper delivered at the 66th Annual Meeting of the American Political Science Association, Los Angeles, September, 1970), p. 3.

4. Fenno, *Power of the Purse,* p. 668. It is worth noting John Manley's observation in *The Politics of Finance: The House Committee on Ways and Means* (Boston: Little, Brown, 1970), pp. 293–94: "House conferees have usually spent more time studying the legislation and probably know the details better than the Senators, who, after all, have more demands on their time than House members. But although technical ability and staff assistance enter into the decisions of conference committees and may give the House some advantage, an understanding of the policies at stake does not necessarily require the ability to answer all the objections to those policies. If the House does better than the Senate in some cases, and if the Senate does better than the House in other cases, the explanation probably lies more in the policy preferences of those involved in the legislation—including extra-congressional groups and individuals—than the substantive expertise or lack of it of the conferees."

5. Fenno, *Power of the Purse,* p. 662.

It is thus quite possible that the findings of both studies accurately reflect the general pattern of conference settlements obtaining during these two different time periods. If this were the case, it would be suggestive of a trend toward greater Senate influence in appropriations conferences, and perhaps other areas.

In *House vs. Senate,* Jeffrey Pressman critically analyzes Steiner's treatment of appropriations conferences and rejects his conclusions:

> Actually, the observation of House "predominance" in these appropriations conferences stems largely from Steiner's selection of conferences.
>
> The Senate prohibition amendment, which was proposed in 1928, merely represented an attempt by a "wet" Senator to embarrass the "drys" by forcing them to vote on an exorbitant sum for enforcement. Thus, the amendment was never expected to be retained in conference; House victory was assured.
>
> In the 1933 bill, House conferees were again successful—this time in limiting the amount to be appropriated for veterans' pensions. But in this case, the House was aided by the prestige and pressure which flowed from the White House.
>
> Finally, in 1943, the House won on the anti-subversion rider because the Senators were unwilling to provoke an argument which would delay the appropriation of desperately needed agency funds.
>
> Thus, it would seem that Steiner's results do not justify an assertion of House predominance in appropriations conferences. For, in his examples, special circumstances assured House victories (pp. 60–61).

It should be noted, in defense of Steiner's study, that it is difficult to locate conferences concerned with major legislation yet totally devoid of "special circumstances." For if we rule out events and influences originating from outside the conference system, such as pressure from the White House, a study of the conference decision will always be incomplete. Similarly, if we exclude from study all conferences characterized by one house's packing a bill with "bargaining" amendments, by the presence of external pressure from the executive branch, interest groups, and other constituencies, or by the necessity of meeting appropriation deadlines, then our sample of conferences would indeed be small and would tend to exclude important legislation.

Pressman's critique is perhaps most helpful in its emphasizing the small number of cases on which Steiner's generalization regarding House dominance is based. We would tend to have more confidence in Fenno's later findings, if only because they are based on the study of 331, rather than 5, appropriations conferences. This study focuses on 268 conferences in which one house prevailed.

Before discussing these findings, however, we should acknowledge the problems involved in measuring conference output in terms of house dominance. When we conceive of policy output in system terms, it becomes evident that an objective measure of output may be misleading. For the perceptions of the conferees in this system are what determine the effect that the output will have on the legislative system as a whole. If we objectively measure conference decisions in one area and find that the conference bills are generally closer to the Senate position, and if the senators perceive these conference settlements as generally closer to the bill originally proposed by the House, it is the second phenomenon which is the more important in terms of understanding the interactions of the House and Senate conferees. The attitudes and actions of those in the system will be determined by their perceptions of reality and not by an unperceived, yet objectively measurable, reality.

On the other hand, we encounter measurement error if we rely solely on the sources of perceptions of senators and representatives. If we look to the *Congressional Record* to determine these perceptions we find distortions such as those produced by a conference chairman attempting to convince his colleagues in the chamber that a particular settlement represents a major victory for that house. Interviews of conference participants, while certainly an important tool in studying conferences, are also subject to the effects of selective perception and selective retention.

Certainly, to make causal inferences regarding conference decisions we would have to rely on both objective measures of chamber dominance and measures of perception of senators and representatives. Prior to this, however, there lies the problem of description of conference decisions. The present study seeks to make general statements about "who wins" in conference in order to provide some basis for the investigation of "how" and "why."

The prominent target for political scientists seeking to attack the problems of measuring policy output has been that of expenditures. As in the case of appropriations conferences, expenditures provide an objective measure in a form permitting relatively easy interpretation and manipulation. Fenno was able to determine which chamber won in conference by comparing the total conference appropriation with that in the House and Senate bills. But even in this relatively uncomplicated area, the pitfalls of measurement error are present:

If, for example, one group is willing to give up an item costing $50 million to get some especially valued item costing $10 million, then dollars and cents measures will be inadequate to define "winning." [6]

When we investigate conferences not involving appropriations the problem of determining who won becomes more complex. For even the particular wording used in the conference bill may mean many things to many men:

> If the House managers objected to a particular phrase, Gross went to a thesaurus and juggled words around until he hit on a verbal equivalent. The fact that both sides were ultimately satisfied with most of the compromises made during the conference struggle cannot be understood without an appreciation of this technique.
>
> The House managers believed that real Senate concessions were being made with every change in language; the Senate sponsors were satisfied that a rose by any other name smells as sweet. [7]

In this study, conferences were coded as closer to the House or Senate bill by relying one the reported conference decision as it was presented in *The Congressional Quarterly*. Only cases in which the conference decision was reported in terms of relative House and Senate influence were included in this part of the study. [8] Appendix A, containing citations from *The Congressional Quarterly*, illustrates the phrasing relied on for the classification of House or Senate victories.

Measurement of House or Senate victories by this method tends to ignore certain important aspects of conference, such as the intensity of the two sides in a particular conflict. It does, however, have the advantage of minimizing the effects of biased coding resulting from the projection and anticipation of a trend. The measurement procedure followed, while it is not as accurate or comprehensive as we would wish, seems to have the advantage of being free from the subjective influences of the researcher.

6. *Ibid.*, p. 661.

7. Stephen K. Bailey, *Congress Makes a Law* (New York: Random House, Vintage Books, 1964), p. 224.

8. The code for this item was as follows: Conference bill closest to bill as passed: (1) House; (2) Senate; (3) split the difference; (4) conferees reported completely new bill; (5) unable to tell or not reported in *The Congressional Quarterly;* (6) no conference agreement reached. That there is some bias in relying on this source cannot be denied. Just as interviews and quantifiable measures lead to some distortion, so too does reliance on a source designed for media use. It is expected, however, that this bias would not favor one chamber over the other, but rather might tend to emphasize the extent of conflict involved in conference. Even interviews tend to display this emphasis on conflict, however. See the comments of Paletz in "Influence in Congress," p. 5 n.

The Pattern of Senate Dominance

When we consider the conferences included in this study in terms of patterns of one-house dominance, we find a pattern similar to that discovered by Fenno in the area of appropriations. Figure 2 indicates a pattern of Senate victories in conference which is even more marked than the earlier pattern of House dominance noted by Steiner.

FIGURE 2. WINNING IN CONFERENCE (N = 297)

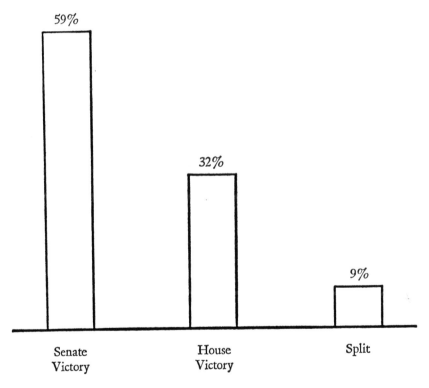

If we eliminate those conferences which produced a compromise bill splitting the difference between the two chambers' positions, we find the general pattern of winning in conference to be exactly that of the appropriations conferences studied by Fenno. Of those conferences in which one or the other house's position prevailed, 65% were won by the Senate and 35% by the House.

As Table 9 shows, this pattern of Senate dominance in conference is a consistent one extending over all of the congresses studied. The variation in this pattern seems to reflect party differences. When the Republicans controlled both houses of Congress, there was a tendency for the percentage of Senate victories to increase. Even a partial explanation as to why Senate dominance is stronger in Republican congresses than in Democratic congresses would require the consideration of many variables beyond the scope of the present study.

One may speculate that this pattern is a reflection of the Senate Republican leadership being more formalized, institutionalized, and decentralized than the Senate Democratic leadership.[9] This could lead to the Republican Senate leadership having more control over the conference bargaining than the Democratic Senate leadership. Before one could offer even tentative explanatory hypotheses, however, comparative study of party leadership in the two chambers would be required. The pattern of increased Senate dominance in Republican congresses can only be noted here. Explanations of the relation of this pattern to other measures of party influence in Congress, and what it means in terms of generalized patterns of legislative behavior, must await further study.

The fact that the House wins more conferences in a Democratic Congress than in a Republican one might also be a reflection of the longer tenure of the Democrats as the majority party. It was suggested in Chapter III that such tenure could lead to functional specification as reflected in greater reliance on subcommittees. This, in turn, would lead to the House conferees in a Democratic Congress being more specialized and informed in a particular area than would be the case in a Republican Congress. The greater number of House victories in a Democratic Congress could be a reflection of these increased resources of influence which House conferees enjoy when the Democrats control Congress.

Since the Senate bill in a House-Senate confrontation is generally perceived as being the more liberal of the two measures (especially on appropriations measures), we could interpret the increased House strength in a Democratic Congress as being related to the influence of southern Democrats in the House committee system. The greater impact of the seniority system in the House, in terms of committee chairmanships and

9. Donald R. Matthews, *U.S. Senators and Their World* (New York: Random House, Vintage Books, 1960), p. 124.

TABLE 9

PATTERNS OF DOMINANCE IN CONFERENCE BY CONGRESS AND MAJORITY PARTY

| | CONGRESS | | | | | MAJORITY PARTY | |
	79th (N = 42)	80th (N = 47)	83d (N = 59)	88th (N = 49)	89th (N = 71)	Democratic (N = 162)	Republican (N = 106)
Senate victory	55%	70%	71%	69%	59%	61%	71%
House victory	45	30	29	31	41	39	29

the resultant increase in the strength of southern Democrats, could have the effect of House conferees successfully resisting a settlement which favored the more liberal Senate measure.[10] All of these tentative explanations of differences related to party control of Congress are offered here only as hypotheses which future studies might refine and test. Answers to most of the questions raised are outside the boundaries of the present study.

Patterns of One-House Dominance in Particular Policy Areas

Steiner's finding that the pattern of House dominance in conference was reversed in the area of fiscal policy suggests consideration of the conferences included here in the same terms. The eight policy categories employed by *The Congressional Quarterly* were used, because they eliminated any problems arising from the researcher's determining in which category a particular conference belongs.[11]

Looking at Figure 3, we find that the area of greatest Senate influence is that of appropriations. The number of appropriations conferences won by the Senate (78%) is higher than that found by Fenno, and this suggests a pattern of Senate dominance in stark contrast to Steiner's earlier findings suggesting House dominance in this area. Fenno hypothesizes that the great difference between the two houses in terms of winning appropriations conferences is best explained by the differing relationships between the two appropriations committees and their respective chambers:

> When the Senate conferees go to the conference room, they not only represent the Senate—they are the Senate. The position they defend will have been worked out with a maximum of participation by Senate members and will enjoy a maximum of support in that body. And the bill will

10. Daniel M. Berman, *In Congress Assembled: The Legislative Process in National Government*, 2d ed. (New York: Macmillan, 1966), p. 131: "Although the seniority system is used in both chambers, its impact is greater in the House that it is in the Senate, for the proportion of one party congressional districts is higher than the proportion of one party states."

11. The eight categories are agriculture, appropriations, education and welfare, foreign policy, general government, national security, public works and resources, and taxes and economic policy. Steiner's classification was as follows: agriculture, appropriations, business and commerce, fiscal policy, government administration, government and politics, labor and employment, national security, revenue, and welfare and social security.

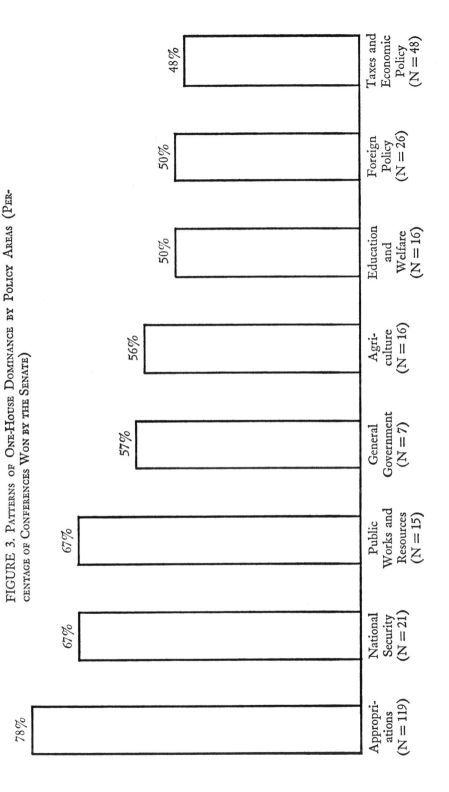

FIGURE 3. PATTERNS OF ONE-HOUSE DOMINANCE BY POLICY AREAS (PERCENTAGE OF CONFERENCES WON BY THE SENATE)

be defended in conference by men who are the leaders not just of the Committee, but of the Senate.

The structural differentiation between the House of Representatives and its Appropriations Committee is much greater than obtains in the Senate. Conflict between the House and the House committee is common, albeit sporadic, and a number of clearly discernible points of tension exist between them.

Decision making inside the Committee is more hierarchically organized than is the case in the Senate, thus conferring considerable influence on a few individuals, while leaving support for them among House members problematical.[12]

In addition to findings supporting those of Fenno in appropriations conferences, we find that the House won over half of the conferences in the area of taxes and economic policy only. Recognizing the limits of comparability generated by the fact that this area is more comprehensive than Steiner's fiscal policy area, it should be noted that the House influence in this area contrasts with that found by Steiner in fiscal policy, but supports his finding of House dominance in the area of taxes.

It was somewhat surprising to find the House and Senate relatively equal in conference victories in the area of foreign policy. Because of the Senate's greater responsibilities in this area, it was expected that Senate conferees would be more influential in the bargaining session. The actual House-Senate split in this area could be interpreted as a reflection of the increasing House role in foreign policy as a result of its activities in the area of foreign aid. If this were the case, it is assumed that this trend

---

12. Fenno, *Power of the Purse*, p. 669. John Manley looks to extracongressional variables to explain why the Senate bill was closer to the final bill than was the House version for fourteen of the twenty major revenue bills he studied for this purpose: "The reason the Senate does better in cases of conflict with the Ways and Means Committee is because politically Senate decisions are more in line with the demands of interest groups, lobbyists, and constituents than House decisions. Ways and Means decisions, made under the closed rule, tend to be less popular with relevant publics than Senate decisions. Some Ways and Means decisions suppose that the Senate will respond favorably to extra-congressional demands, but the job of Ways and Means, as the members see it, is to balance the fiscal realities with the plethora of demands for tax reductions or special provisions. This sometimes means denying popular demands, rejecting demands made by those who are attuned to the tax-making process, leaving such matters to the Senate, or postponing such matters to members' bill time. The items in dispute between the House and Senate, therefore, tend to have strong interest group–lobbyist support or wide appeal to the electorate, and it is almost inevitable that some will survive the conference committee" (*The Politics of Finance*, p. 279). Manley's comprehensive study finds Senate predominance in this area, contrary to the findings reported here and to the perceptions of most members of Ways and Means. An excellent discussion of the problems associated with measuring conference victories is found on pages 269–72 of his study.

would be indicated by an increasing number of House victories in foreign policy conferences over the twenty-year period covered in this study.

In order to determine whether such a trend exists in foreign and other policy areas, the pattern of one-house dominance in policy areas was studied for each of the five congresses. Figure 4 shows this breakdown by congresses.

Before discussing some of the patterns reflected in Figure 4, we should emphasize the fact that controlling for both policy area and Congress produces a distribution with a small number of cases in each category. The small samples not only partially account for the extreme variation between congresses, but also greatly limit our interpreting these patterns as reflections of general trends. The breakdown by congresses is required if we are to discover changes over time, but such a method also has the effect of greatly magnifying slight differences between congresses.

Recognizing these great limitations, we may turn our attention to some of the patterns revealed by this study. In the area of appropriations, with the exception of the 83d Congress, there does seem to be a trend toward increasing Senate dominance in this area. There is no overlap between this study, which begins with conferences in 1945, and Steiner's earlier study, which included one conference in the 1930's and one in the 1940's. Thus it is quite possible that the present Senate dominance in the area of appropriations is a recent phenomenon, becoming pronounced only in the last twenty years.[13]

Foreign policy conferences do not present such a clear pattern. The expectation that House victories in this area are a reflection of House influence in foreign aid, and that this would be indicated by an increase in House victories over this period, is not borne out by the pattern of winning in foreign policy conferences. Indeed, the point of lowest Senate influence is found in the 79th Congress, which begins the period studied.

During periods of Republican control, the Senate was more successful in foreign policy, winning 58% of these conferences. The lower figure of Senate victories (43%) when the Democrats controlled both houses is greatly influenced by the large number of House victories in the 79th Congress.

Any general statement about relative chamber influence in the area of foreign policy, however, would require a more detailed study of these

13. House resentment over the Senate's increasing influence in the appropriations process was one of the major factors involved in the celebrated Cannon-Hayden dispute of 1962. See Pressman, *House vs. Senate,* pp. 80–97.

FIGURE 4. PATTERNS OF ONE-HOUSE DOMINANCE IN PARTICULAR POLICY AREAS BY CONGRESS (PERCENTAGE OF CONFERENCES WON BY THE SENATE)

1. Agriculture

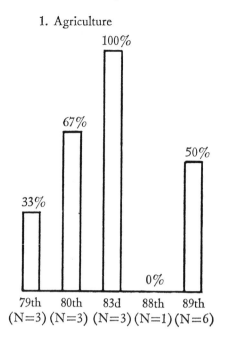

2. Appropriations

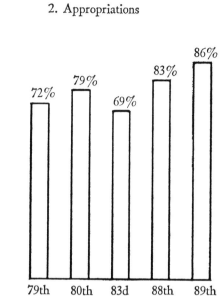

3. Education and Welfare

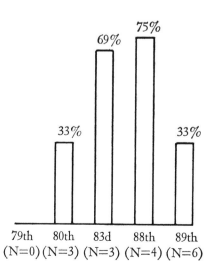

4. Foreign Policy

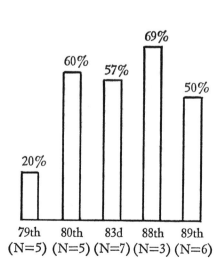

5. General Government

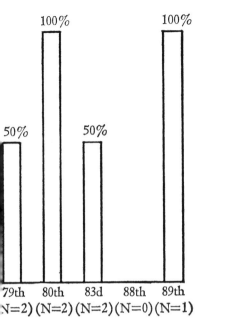

100%

100%

50% 50%

79th 80th 83d 88th 89th
(N=2) (N=2) (N=2) (N=0) (N=1)

6. National Security

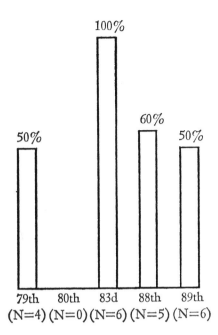

100%

60%

50% 50%

79th 80th 83d 88th 89th
(N=4) (N=0) (N=6) (N=5) (N=6)

7. Public Works and Resources

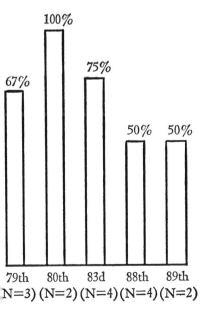

100%

75%

67%

50% 50%

79th 80th 83d 88th 89th
(N=3) (N=2) (N=4) (N=4) (N=2)

8. Taxes and Economic Policy

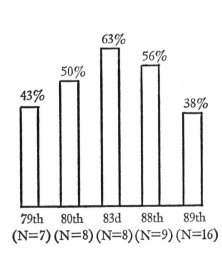

63%

56%

50%

43%

38%

79th 80th 83d 88th 89th
(N=7) (N=8) (N=8) (N=9) (N=16)

conferences and consideration of such other variables as party positions and the influence of the President in these conferences.

The patterns of influence represented in the other policy areas certainly do not suggest clear trends of increasing or decreasing predominance on the part of one chamber. Analysis of relative influence in these policy areas would best be accomplished through extensive case studies which considered the particular influences acting on these conferences during a particular Congress. The focus on general trends in conference decisions and the methods employed to locate such trends in this study preclude such a particularized investigation of conferences in each policy area.

Patterns of One-House Dominance in Intercommittee Subsystems

Fenno's observation that the explanation for Senate dominance in appropriations conferences is to be found in the differing structural characteristics of the two committees and their relationships to the parent chambers suggests that a study of conference outcomes in terms of the relevant standing committees might be a productive avenue of research. Conference committees may be conceived more precisely as intercommittee bargaining structures than as intercameral structures. In some areas, this reduction to subsystem analysis may be carried even further, as is indicated by Pressman's comment on appropriations conferences:

> Conferences are really confrontations between pairs of House and Senate subcommittees considering a piece of legislation, and the relationships between various sets of subcommittees differ widely from each other.
>
> Some subcommittee sets (like Defense) are well-known for the cordiality prevailing between Senate and House groups, while others (like Legislative Appropriations) have often been the focal points for severe conflict.[14]

This study does not attempt to analyze patterns of winning in terms of subcommittees primarily because of the sacrifice of generality resulting from the small number of cases in each subcommittee set. The absence of subcommittees on the Ways and Means and Senate Finance committees, and the presence of some subcommittees with no established and

14. *Ibid.*, p. 61.

persistent areas of jurisdiction, also limits consideration of conferences in terms of subcommittee sets.

The best method for comparing relative House and Senate conference influence in terms of committees would be to consider the conference in terms of House and Senate committee sets. Thus, conferences in the House Ways and Means Committee–Senate Finance Committee set would be studied as a group. A problem arises, however, because of differing patterns of allocation of legislation to standing committees. Consideration of the Commerce Committee set, for example, is hindered by the fact that a conference bill might have been handled by the Commerce Committee in the Senate, whereas in the House the Agriculture Committee had jurisdiction.

Because of this problem, it was decided to consider the two houses separately in order to determine patterns of conference success across the different standing committees. There is an obvious association between the patterns in the two houses, and after looking at the distribution in each house we shall consider some of these findings in terms of inter-committee sets. Figures 5 and 6 present the findings relating to conference success of the standing committees in the two chambers.

A caveat is in order, again, regarding the effect of the small samples in certain categories. This is perhaps most obvious when we look at conference bills going through the Government Operations Committees. Two conference bills in this particular sample were routed through the House Government Operations Committee. Of these two bills, only one was handled by the Senate Government Operations Committee. In the latter case the conference settlement was a Senate victory, and this leads to the statement that the Senate Government Operations Committee was successful in 100% of its conferences. As Figure 6 indicates, however, the second conference settlement favored the House position, and this is expressed in terms of the House Government Operations Committee being successful in 50% of the conferences studied. In spite of the great distortions in this case, and because the larger number of cases in the other categories reduces the effect of such exaggerations, it was decided to include the Government Operations Committee, if only to make the description more complete.

Looking at Figure 5, we see that the pronounced superiority of the Senate in obtaining conference settlements similar to its position does not hold for five of its sixteen committees. The Senate Labor and Public Welfare, Foreign Relations, Judiciary, Commerce, and Interior commit-

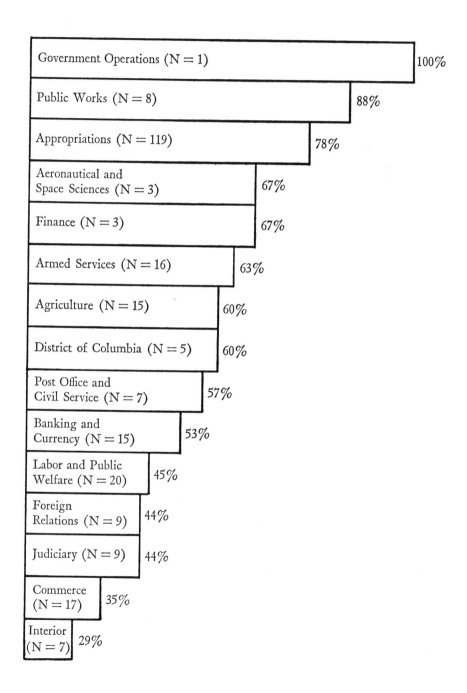

FIGURE 5. Senate Committees and Dominance in Conference (Percentage of Conferences Won by the Senate)

FIGURE 6. House Committees and Dominance in Conference (Percentage of Conferences Won by the House)

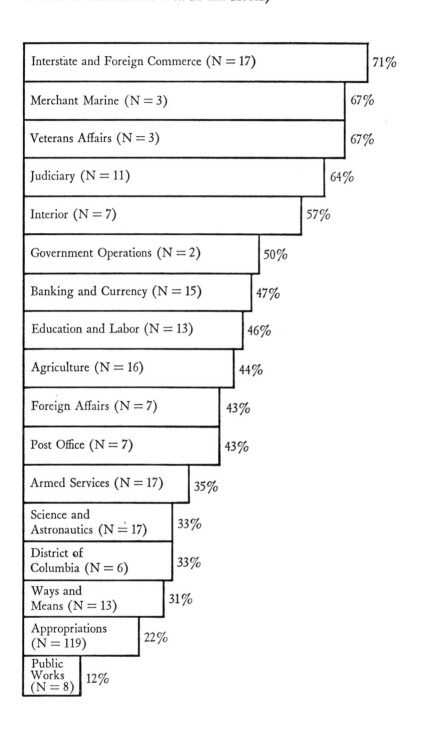

Interstate and Foreign Commerce (N = 17)   71%

Merchant Marine (N = 3)   67%

Veterans Affairs (N = 3)   67%

Judiciary (N = 11)   64%

Interior (N = 7)   57%

Government Operations (N = 2)   50%

Banking and Currency (N = 15)   47%

Education and Labor (N = 13)   46%

Agriculture (N = 16)   44%

Foreign Affairs (N = 7)   43%

Post Office (N = 7)   43%

Armed Services (N = 17)   35%

Science and Astronautics (N = 17)   33%

District of Columbia (N = 6)   33%

Ways and Means (N = 13)   31%

Appropriations (N = 119)   22%

Public Works (N = 8)   12%

tees have lost to their House counterparts in conference more often than they have won.

Figure 6, showing eleven of seventeen House committees losing to the Senate in over half their conferences, confirms this general pattern of overwhelming Senate success in conference.[15] Only the Interstate and Foreign Commerce, Merchant Marine, Veterans Affairs, Judiciary, and Interior committees demonstrated a pattern of strong House influence on the conference committee.[16]

We may interpret Figure 5 as suggesting that Senate conferees from the Public Works, Appropriations, Aeronautical and Space Sciences, and Finance committees are extremely influential in dealing with the other chamber in order to obtain a conference settlement closer to the Senate-passed bill. Conferees from the Senate Armed Services, Agriculture, District of Columbia, and Post Office committees also tend to achieve a conference bill favoring the Senate position, although their influence does not seem to be as great as that of colleagues from the aforementioned committees.

Similarly, Figure 6 suggests that House conferees from the Interstate and Foreign Commerce, Merchant Marine, Veterans Affairs, Judiciary, and Interior committees are generally more successful in obtaining a favorable conference settlement than are House conferees from the other standing committees.

By once again conceiving of conferences as being part of the inter-committee subsystems of the legislature, and on the basis of patterns illustrated in the preceding figures, we are able to make general state-

15. The House Rules, Un-American Activities, and House Administration committees handled none of the conference bills studied; the first-mentioned committee was, of course, a procedural rather than a substantive committee.

16. The fact that both houses are shown as winning fewer than half of the conferences of the Senate Foreign Relations Committee and the House Foreign Affairs Committee might raise some academic eyebrows. It will be recalled that the study of policy areas revealed a fifty-fifty split between the two chambers' success in the area of foreign policy. The number of cases in this area was twenty-six, whereas the number of cases going through the respective committees was nine for Senate Foreign Relations and seven for House Foreign Affairs. This drop in the sample from the area of foreign policy is produced by the fact that some bills classified by *The Congressional Quarterly* as being foreign policy bills are not handled by these two committees. Bills dealing with immigration, for instance, are classified as foreign policy bills, but are generally handled by the judiciary committees.

The different samples in the two chambers' committees are produced by cases such as the one where the House Banking and Currency Committee and the Senate Foreign Relations Committee were the bodies handling the bill concerning U.S. participation in the Inter-American Development Bank. The 44% Senate and the 43% House victories in this area may best be interpreted as a relatively even split between the two committees in terms of conference influence.

ments about the relative influence of the House and Senate members of the subsystem, and to predict, *ceteris paribus,* which chamber's position the output of the conference will resemble. Table 10 is presented as an outline of relative chamber influence in the intercommittee subsystems.

TABLE 10
RELATIVE HOUSE AND SENATE INFLUENCE IN THE INTERCOMMITTEE SUBSYSTEMS OF CONGRESS

INTERCOMMITTEE SUBSYSTEM		CHAMBER BILL CONFERENCE SETTLEMENT MOST RESEMBLES
Senate Committee	House Committee	
Aeronautical and Space Sciences	Science and Astronautics	Senate
Agriculture	Agriculture	Senate
Appropriations	Appropriations	Senate
Armed Services	Armed Services	Senate
Banking and Currency	Banking and Currency	Both chambers
Commerce	Interstate and Foreign Commerce	House
District of Columbia	District of Columbia	Senate
Finance	Ways and Means	Senate
Foreign Relations	Foreign Affairs	Both chambers
Government Operations	Government Operations	Both chambers
Interior and Insular Affairs	Interior and Insular Affairs	House
Judiciary	Judiciary	House
Labor and Public Welfare	Education and Labor	Both chambers
Post Office and Civil Service	Post Office and Civil Service	Senate
Public Works	Public Works	Senate

Because it measures only the conference outcomes of these subsystems, it is necessarily an incomplete description of these intercommittee structures. The interactions of House and Senate committee and subcommittee members, legislative staff, interest group representatives, and officers of the executive branch produce legislative output in the form of a conference bill. We have only obliquely measured the positions of the House and Senate managers and evaluated the conference output in terms of the stated positions of the two chambers; we have not observed the interactions of the other actors in this subsystem, nor have we evaluated the output in terms of their influence. Table 10 actually tells us very little about the total legislative system and its component subsystems. The general outline is presented here, not as a definitive statement, but rather as a possible source of speculation and an initiator of more thorough studies.

A perusal of this outline of relative chamber influence in conference subsystems leads to speculation as to why one chamber would be dominant in a particular area. In seeking to delineate factors which might be considered in such studies, we can focus on two broad areas for research. The first is the description and identification of all the actors in this subsystem and the study of the positions and interactions of all these elements. This would require consideration of interest group and executive agency representatives as well as legislators. It would necessitate studying the conferees' electoral, legislative, and executive constituencies in order to determine patterns of linkage. All of these factors would have to be considered in terms of the conference situation and its environment, for we would expect the legislators' sources of both influence and information to be quite different in a conference situation than they are in a floor vote, or even a committee situation.

The second area is that which focuses on the relationship between a standing committee and its parent chamber. Fenno's study suggests that this relationship is an important factor in determining the relative influence of conferees in the intercommittee subsystem. Research in this area would focus on such factors as the autonomy of committee decision-making and the relative specialization and prestige associated with a particular committee.

Looking again at Table 10, we observe that House conferees are relatively successful in the commerce, interior, and judiciary subsystems. Scrutiny of some of the conferences included in these samples indicated that House victories may in some cases be attributed to the differing constituencies of senators and representatives. A member of the House might justifiably be more concerned with legislation establishing a national park or forest in his district than is a senator from the same state.[17] Similarly, a representative may be more vulnerable to pressures from local business interests concerned with the effects of legislation in the commerce sub-

17. This point suggests that a study of legislators' perceptions as to constituency attitudes about the relative influence of the district's congressman and the state's senators in securing such federal programs for the district and the state might indicate the importance of such projects to members of the two chambers. If the district's representative is perceived as being generally responsible for the success or failure of securing such projects, this could lead to his being more adamant about retaining such measures in conference than are senators.

system than are senators whose larger constituencies dilute the effects of single-interest group influence.

A House conference victory in such cases would be more correctly conceived as a victory for the interest groups concerned. The conference situation itself seems to offer great opportunity for the exertion of outside influence. As Professor Berman has noted:

> At no other point in the congressional process can so little be learned about why actions are taken and by whom they are promoted.
> This situation is made to order for a lobbyist, either from an executive agency or a private organization. He has only a small number of congressmen on whom to work, he knows that what they decide cannot be effectively challenged, and he has an atmosphere of secrecy in which to campaign. Because of the absence of publicity, conferees need not fear being held accountable for what they do.[18]

In describing some of these conferences as House victories, then, we are dealing with an intervening variable of relative chamber influence. In some cases, the conference settlement may reflect not just a victory for the House, but rather a victory for the other actors in the subsystem or a victory for outside groups exerting influence through the House conferees.

To illustrate this point, let us consider one of the Interior bills included in this sample, S.4, establishing the National Wilderness Preservation System in 1964. In this study we refer to the conference settlement as being a victory for the House. Another political scientist, having studied the legislative history of this bill in much greater detail, comments, "In the conference committee, adjustments generally favorable to the mining and timber interests were secured by House conferees." [19]

To attempt to explain why the House or the Senate is more successful in any one area, then, would require consideration of many more variables than are included here. Since this study does permit a discussion of general trends in relative chamber influence in conference, we can determine that House conferees tend to be consistently successful in the commerce, interior, and judiciary subsystems. In order to explain why this is the case, however, we would have to include many more actors in the subsystem studied, and then approach the problem through individual case studies.

---

18. Berman, *In Congress Assembled*, p. 311.
19. Robert S. Gilmour, "Policy Making for the National Forests" (Ph.D. diss., Columbia University, 1968), p. 345.

Looking at conference output in terms of the relationships between the standing committee and its parent chamber, we are able to discuss one aspect of this interdependence. Fenno observed that Senate conferees are influential in appropriations conferences, in part, because they go to a conference backed by a strong consensus in their own chamber. It

TABLE 11

RELATIVE PRESTIGE OF HOUSE AND SENATE COMMITTEES CONSTITUTING THE CONFERENCE SUBSYSTEMS

House Committee	Rank	Rank	Senate Committee
Ways and Means	1	2	Finance
Appropriations	2	5	Appropriations
Foreign Affairs	3	1	Foreign Relations
Armed Services	4	6	Armed Services
Interstate and Foreign Commerce	5	3	Commerce
Judiciary	6	4	Judiciary
Agriculture	7	7	Agriculture
Education and Labor	8	10	Labor and Public Welfare
Banking and Currency	9	9	Banking and Currency
Public Works	10	11	Public Works
Post Office and Civil Service	11	13	Post Office and Civil Service
Science and Astronautics	12	15	Astronautical and Space Sciences
District of Columbia	13	14	District of Columbia
Interior and Insular Affairs	14	8	Interior and Insular Affairs
Government Operations	15	12	Government Operations

SOURCE: Adapted from Malcolm Jewell and Samuel Patterson, *The Legislative Process in the United States* (New York: Random House, 1966), p. 206.
NOTE: Adjustments were made in excluding the House Rules, Un-American Activities, House Administration, Merchant Marine, and Veterans Affairs committees and the Senate Rules and Administration Committee. The committee rank refers to its order of desirability as reflected in patterns of committee transfers. Sources here include: George Goodwin, Jr., "The Seniority System in Congress," *American Political Science Review*, LIII (June, 1959), 433; Nicholas A. Masters, "Committee Assignments in the U.S. House of Representatives," *APSR*, LV (June, 1961), 353; and Donald R. Matthews, *U.S. Senators and Their World*, pp. 148 ff.

would also seem that one element of the relationship between a standing committee and its parent body would be reflected in the relative prestige which that committee enjoys in its chamber. We might speculate that conferees from a highly prestigious committee would go to a conference more certain of their chamber's support than would conferees from a standing committee with less prestige.

Such an observation is not easily translated into a testable hypothesis, however, because of the fact that conferees from both chambers may come from highly prestigious committees in their respective chambers. Other things being equal, we might expect conferees from the prestigious Ways and Means Committee to be successful in conference because of the support they enjoy in the House as a whole. When we realize that their Senate counterparts come from the highly prestigious Finance Committee, however, it is clear that other things, in this case, are not equal. A prediction of conference success based on the relative standing of the committee from which conferees are drawn tells us little about conferences which draw on equally prestigious committees in the two chambers.

In order to provide a standard of comparison, the relative prestige of the House and Senate committees which make up the various conference subsystems was determined. On the basis of the relative committee ranks presented in Table 11, each conference subsystem was classified in terms of whether the House committee involved was ranked higher or lower than its corresponding Senate committee as to prestige in the respective chambers. This relative prestige ranking was then related to House victories in conference in order to determine the relationship between committee prestige and success in conference.

Table 12 suggests that there is a relationship between committee prestige and success in conference. The pattern, however, is in the opposite direction from that expected. House conferees drawn from committees with lower prestige than that of the Senate committees involved in conference were generally more successful than were House conferees from committees with prestige rankings above those of their Senate counterparts.[20]

This pattern reflects the fact that the House committees which were generally successful in conference included the low-ranking Merchant Marine, Veterans Affairs, Interior, and Government Operations com-

20. Separate tests were also performed for each chamber individually. In the House, this same pattern relating low committee prestige with success in conference obtained. In the Senate, higher prestige was positively associated with success in conference.

TABLE 12

RELATIONSHIP BETWEEN HOUSE COMMITTEE PRESTIGE AND VICTORY IN
CONFERENCE *

	PRESTIGE OF HOUSE COMMITTEE		
	Lower than Senate (N = 39)	Same as Senate (N = 31)	Higher than Senate (N = 197)
House victory	62%	45%	35%
Senate victory	38	55	65

* $x^2 = 17.17$, 2DF; significance level = .001.

mittees. Thus, a study testing the relationship between committee prestige
and conference success is somewhat contaminated by the independent
variable's measurement tapping other dimensions along with committee
prestige.

The findings here suggest rejection of the general hypothesis that high
committee prestige is positively related to success of that committee's
representatives in conference. They do not, however, justify an assertion
that the relationship between a committee and its parent chamber has
little effect on the conference outcome. Our measure of this relationship
has been extremely crude, and we have not considered other factors involved in the relationship between committee and chamber, such as the
degree of specialization involved in committee work and the decision-
making autonomy which the committee enjoys vis-à-vis other committees
and the chamber as a whole. Fenno's observation that the chamber-
committee relationship greatly influences the conference outcome in
appropriations remains a guide to speculation in other areas and a worthwhile object of continued study.

Conference Representation and Patterns of Dominance

This discussion has suggested that the particular standing committees
involved in handling a conference bill are important factors in determining conference outcome. In Chapters II and III we focused on the variables of party representation and the representation of supporters of a

particular bill in conference. Although specific factors are most important in explaining conference decisions, we return to certain variables of representation on the conference delegations to try again to determine general patterns relating these variables to conference output.

In discussing party representation, we should emphasize again the caveat regarding the many assumptions involved when dealing with party representation in general terms. Acknowledging that any general study of this type tends to blur the distinction between partisan and non-partisan issues, we can still ask whether patterns of minority party representation in conference seem to make any difference in terms of which chamber is more successful in conference. Tables 13 and 14 repre-

TABLE 13

RELATIONSHIP BETWEEN MINORITY REPRESENTATION ON HOUSE DELEGATIONS AND HOUSE VICTORIES IN CONFERENCE *

	Index of Representation of Minority Party on House Conference Delegation			
	Less than .9 (N = 81)	.9 to .99 (N = 104)	1.0 to 1.09 (N = 36)	1.1 and over (N = 47)
House victory	28%	37%	39%	40%
Senate victory	72	63	61	60

* Kendall's tau = −0.0976; Z = −2.38; significance level = .01.

sent attempts to answer this question.

An interpretation of the patterns reflected in Tables 13 and 14 must be undertaken with caution. It will be recalled that a Republican majority tended to underrepresent the minority party on conference in both chambers (Table 4). In this chapter, we discovered that the Senate tended to be more successful in conference during Republican congresses than during Democratic congresses (Table 9). Thus, greater Senate success when the minority party is underrepresented in both delegations is, at least in part, due to the interrelationships existing among all of these variables. Our measure of party representation, then, is not a true measure of independent variation, but rather one which includes variation influenced by Republican or Democratic control of the Congress.

TABLE 14

RELATIONSHIP BETWEEN MINORITY PARTY REPRESENTATION ON SENATE
DELEGATIONS AND SENATE VICTORIES IN CONFERENCE *

| | Index of Representation of Minority Party on Senate Conference Delegation | | | |
	Less than .9 (N = 108)	.9 to .99 (N = 59)	1.0 to 1.09 (N = 54)	1.1 and over (N = 47)
House victory	30%	34%	35%	49%
Senate victory	70	66	65	51

* Kendall's tau = 0.1327; Z = −3.24; significance level = .001.

We find the two chambers to be quite different in terms of the effects of party representation on conference output. In the House, conference delegations which overrepresented the minority party tended to be more successful than those which underrepresented that party. Although the differences are generally small, the direction of the relationship is a consistent one suggesting that overrepresentation of the minority party on House conference delegations does not weaken that delegation's bargaining position in conference.

The opposite pattern obtains in the Senate, where we find that chamber most successful in conferences which underrepresented the minority party. This pattern tends to give credence to the argument that the overrepresentation of the minority party on conference committees tends to give that minority greater influence in the final stage of legislative action and to weaken the Senate's delegation in its bargaining with the House.

Because of the opposite pattern in the House and the relatively small differences in both houses, it would seem that political scientists seeking to explain the relative influence of the two chambers in conference might more profitably investigate factors other than relative party representation in conference. As we have already noted in Chapter II, a study which seeks to describe and explain general patterns of conference activity, not just in cases of party issues, but in all cases, would identify party representation on conference committees as a relatively minor variable affecting the conference decision. It is possible that much of the relationship indicated in these tables is more a function of variables such as the majority party in Congress, the Congress in which a conference occurs, and the standing committees involved, than it is a function of the over-representation of the minority party.

Previous discussion has also indicated that many observers, in discussing party representation in conference, are actually discussing the separate question of the representation of minority opinion in conference. Over-representation of the minority party on conference committees would affect that chamber's influence in conference only if such overrepresentation meant that many conferees did not support the chamber's position on the conference bill.

In order to determine the effects of this representation of the minority position on conference committees, the House and Senate delegations were compared in terms of representation of supporters of a bill, and these patterns of representation were then related to conference output.

Table 15 suggests that the relative supporter representation on the

TABLE 15

RELATIONSHIP BETWEEN REPRESENTATION OF BILL SUPPORTERS AND CONFERENCE VICTORY *

	PROPORTION OF BILL SUPPORTERS ON CHAMBER DELEGATIONS		
	Senate Higher than House (N = 24)	House and Senate Equal (N = 23)	House Higher than Senate (N = 14)
House victory	46%	35%	50%
Senate victory	54	65	50

* Kendall's tau $= -0.0021$; $Z = -0.02$; not significant.
NOTE: The small sample sizes result from the fact that the only conferences included in this study were those in which there was a roll call vote in both the House and the Senate.

House and Senate delegations has little effect on which house wins in conference. Although we may note the fact that the variation in supporter representation and success in conference move in the same direction, the differences are extremely small. The highest percentage of House victories is found in those conferences in which the House delegation had a higher proportion of legislation supporters than did the Senate delegation. But the Senate was most successful when the proportion of supporters on both delegations was the same. Rather than attempting to explain a "pattern" on the basis of such small differences, we might be more correct in interpreting Table 15 as indicating that conference representation of supporters of a bill does not seem to be significantly related to chamber success in conference.

Measurement error, that specter of the social sciences, may again be charged with some of the problems encountered in interpreting the relationships of Table 15. We have relied on the legislator's position on a roll call vote on final passage or recommittal as an indicator of his support or lack of support for his chamber's position on the conference bill. Behind the closed doors of the conference committee, however, a legislator's position might be quite different from one taken in the clear light of a roll call vote. "You certainly get some different attitudes in a conference than you would anticipate by listening to speeches on the floor," observed a congressman in Clapp's study. "There is one senator, for example, who is known primarily for a particular position on foreign aid. Yet in conference I never saw anyone fight more ardently for a different position." [21]

Because of a desire to achieve generality by studying a large number of cases, we have failed to specify certain factors such as those represented by a legislator's voting for a bill, yet having strong reservations about certain sections or amendments which lie at the heart of the conference disagreement. Again, we must recognize the limits of this study and acknowledge the specificity of the case study approach in locating important variables for continued research. However, in this chapter we have located some of the important variables which must be considered in seeking answers to how and why one chamber consistently achieves success in conference, and have perhaps moved the discipline closer to answering Fenno's first question, "Who wins?"

21. Charles L. Clapp, *The Congressman: His Work as He Sees It* (New York: Doubleday, Anchor Books, 1964), p. 284.

V

Conference Bargaining

The essence of bargaining is the communication of intent; the perception of intent; the manipulation of expectations about what one will accept or refuse; the issuance of threats, offers, and assurances; the display of resolve and evidence of capabilities, the communication of constraints on what one can do; the search for compromise and jointly desirable exchanges; the creation of sanctions to enforce understandings and agreements; genuine efforts to persuade and inform; and the creation of hostility, friendliness, mutual respect, or rules of etiquette. The actual talk, especially the formal talk, is only a part of this, often a small part.

—Thomas Schelling

As PART of a continuous, but cautious, movement of political science toward more general theories of behavior, some contemporary political scientists have sought explanations of legislative behavior in general theories of organizations.[1] Such a procedure aids the researcher in collecting, organizing, and analyzing data in his attempt to explain variation in behavior and contributes to the refinement of theory by empirically testing hypotheses. Focusing our attention on particular relationships within organizations as such will increase our understanding of the particular relationships involved in legislative behavior and the specific institution of the Congress.

1. For example, see Lewis A. Froman, Jr., "Organization Theory and the Explanation of Important Characteristics of Congress," *American Political Science Review,* LXII (June, 1968), 518–26; and Robert L. Peabody, "Organization Theory and Legislative Behavior: Bargaining, Hierarchy, and Change in the U.S. House of Representatives" (Paper delivered at the 59th Annual Meeting of the American Political Science Association, New York, 1963).

In this chapter we will look more closely at patterns of conference bargaining. Thirty-four conferences, selected from the larger sample, constitute the data base of this discussion.[2] Rather than outlining the legislative history of each bill and presenting a complete case study of each conference, cases will be used to illustrate certain aspects of conference bargaining. The purpose here is not to provide a complete description of these conferences, but rather to discuss certain patterns of bargaining which these cases suggest.

Organization Theory, Conflict Reduction, and Conference Committees

In their theory of formal organizations, James March and Herbert Simon maintain that any organization reacts to conflict by four major processes: (1) problem-solving; (2) persuasion; (3) bargaining; and (4) "politics."[3] In the case of problem-solving, it is assumed that there are shared objectives, and that a decision can be reached by gathering additional information in order to identify a solution which satisfies the shared objectives. Persuasion is used when there is a difference of individual goals, but, at the same time, a belief that at some level objectives are shared. The conflict over subgoals is thus mediated by reference to common goals.

When there is disagreement over goals, and when that disagreement is taken as fixed, bargaining is the process used for conflict reduction. Bargaining differs from the first two processes chiefly in its seeking to achieve a reduction of conflict within the limits of the given conflict over goals. Actors in a bargaining situation seek to change other actors' behavior without necessarily changing the goals or objectives which partially determine that behavior. "Politics," in the special sense used by March and Simon, refers to the process whereby one or more of the participants seeks to expand the arena of bargaining. This "socialization of conflict"

2. Conferences were selected for more detailed study, not because they were representative but rather because they were deviant cases in which conflict was greater than normally obtains. Such deviant cases were generally more instructive than the normal, low-conflict conference, because the strategies and bargaining activities of those involved tended to be brought into the open. Appendix B lists the bills included in this phase of the study.

3. James March and Herbert Simon, *Organizations* (New York: John Wiley, 1958), pp. 129–31.

generally takes the form of seeking aid from an actor outside the immediate bargaining system.[4]

The processes of problem-solving and persuasion, which represent attempts to reach private as well as public agreement, are collectively referred to as analytic processes by March and Simon. The latter two processes are subsumed under the more general term of bargaining, and identified by the fact that conflict is reduced without changing the difference in goals. In specifying when an organization will use analytic or bargaining processes, the authors suggest that the more organizational conflict resembles individual differences, the greater the use of analytic procedures; the more it reflects intergroup differences, the greater the use of bargaining.

Considering conference interaction in terms of the March-Simon typology draws attention to differences which might otherwise have been unobserved. There is a tendency to speak of all conference interaction as bargaining, without recognizing other processes of conflict reduction. Moreover, the term bargaining itself refers to many different patterns of exchange. Because of its comprehensiveness, any discussion of bargaining in Congress must distinguish among these different patterns if it is to be an accurate representation of legislative behavior.[5]

In studying conference committees, we find that the intercameral conflict often reflects a conflict over goals. At other times there are shared objectives, joint information-gathering, and conflict reduction by problem-solving rather than bargaining. The conference conflict in some cases represents individual conflict in which there is much disagreement within, as well as between, the two houses. In other cases, we find that the conflict more resembles an intergroup conflict between two unified houses. A conference decision is generally reached within the limits of the conference system itself, but appeals for outside intervention are not unique.

Conference Agreement through Analytic Procedures

Problem-solving and persuasion are identified chiefly by the fact that genuine and complete agreement among the principals is achieved. The

4. The term is Schattschneider's, as used in his more general discussion of politics as conflict. See *The Semi-Sovereign People* (New York: Holt, Rinehart and Winston, 1960), pp. 1–19.

5. A good discussion of some of the types of bargaining found in Congress is provided in Lewis A. Froman, Jr., *The Congressional Process* (Boston: Little, Brown, 1967), pp. 22–30.

conference settlement represents not just a mutual adjustment of actions but complete conciliation in terms of goals.

Consideration of conference activity in this manner is complicated by the fact that we are dealing with four principals: the House, the Senate, House conferees, and Senate conferees. We might find, therefore, that House and Senate conferees resolved a conflict through problem-solving, yet there still remains a basic goal conflict between the two chambers in that particular area. Subsequent legislation might reflect this conflict, lead to a bargaining procedure in conference, and suggest that the earlier interpretation of conference activity as problem-solving was inaccurate. Problem-solving connotes a terminal decision, a sort of finality which is nonexistent in the legislative process.

There is, however, variation in the extent of disagreement reflected in conference. In an area such as rivers and harbors legislation we would tend to find relatively high interchamber agreement as to objectives. On the other hand, House and Senate differences in the area of foreign aid usually reflect more general disagreement between the two chambers:

> We went to conference facing a situation where there were not only important differences in the two bills before us, but where there were basic differences between the House and Senate conferees on U.S. foreign policy and on the nature and purpose of our foreign aid program.
> After long negotiation, we have been able to work out compromises with respect to the legislation itself, but I regret to say that disagreement on fundamental issues of policy still remain.[6]

We would be more likely to find analytic solutions in areas where there are not the sort of basic, goal-oriented differences reflected in foreign aid.

By conceiving of this disagreement as a continuum between shared goals and total goal conflict, we may anticipate that some patterns of conference conflict reduction will reflect characteristics of analytic procedures. Even in cases where there are not explicitly common goals, conflict reduction might consist primarily of evocative procedures which seek additional information as a means for settlement.

Analytic procedures are characterized by this search for additional information as a means of reducing conflict. This study suggests that conference settlements at times involve such information-gathering pro-

---

6. House, *Congressional Record*, 89th Cong., 2d sess., 1966, 112, pt. 16, 21620.

cedures. A distinction must be made, however, between two general types of information which influence the conference settlement. Conferees may seek additional technical information in the area of conference legislation. In other instances, the type of information sought may have to do with the positions of interest group or executive branch representatives on the legislation under consideration.

Both types of information are found in conference interaction. Cases which involve information regarding positions of other actors are difficult to distinguish from bargaining procedures which seek to involve outside actors in the conference bargaining system. In some cases this additional information will serve to produce a genuine conciliation regarding means to shared goals, while in others its effect is primarily one of demonstrating outside support for one of the actors in a bargaining situation. Although most of this chapter will be devoted to a discussion of conference interaction as bargaining, it does seem worthwhile to consider some conference activities in terms of analytic procedures of information-seeking.

The search for technical information which will contribute to a conference decision is often manifested by one chamber promising hearings or continued investigation in order to accumulate the necessary material. Although this is, in effect, conflict reduction by delaying a decision, in the immediate conference situation it does produce a conference agreement. One chamber will often refuse to accept the other's provisions in a certain area because of the lack of information regarding their effects, even though both chambers agree on the objectives in that area. Settlement is postponed until the information is available.

In the conferences studied, there was a tendency for House conferees to propose hearings. Senate conferees would agree to delete a Senate provision in exchange for promises that additional information on the matter would be sought through current or future House committee hearings. In the 1964 excise tax cut conference, House conferees succeeded in obtaining a conference decision in their favor by insisting that certain cuts not be made until the House Ways and Means Committee had completed hearings on the effects of such cuts.[7] Reports of the conference settlement on the Supplemental Foreign Assistance Authorization Act of 1966 and the Demonstration Cities Act of 1966 reflect this same pattern:

7. *Congressional Quarterly Almanac,* XX, 1964, 542; and Senate, *Congressional Record,* 88th Cong., 2d sess., 1964, 10, pt. 12, 15443.

Senate conferees agreed to drop the amendment when House conferees promised to consider the principle involved during its hearings on the regular foreign aid bill.[8]

Leading Democrats on the House Housing Subcommittee reportedly influenced the conference decision by promising the program's sponsor, Senator Muskie, that they would hold subcommittee hearings on the (seasonal housing) plan early in the 1967 session.[9]

The cases cited serve only to suggest that analytic procedures are employed in conference conflict reduction. In these instances, the search for additional information, while contributing to a conference decision in the immediate sense, was part of a conflict-reduction procedure extending over more than one conference. One conjectures that much conference interaction, especially in the case of low-conflict conferences, follows a pattern of seeking additional information in order to arrive at a conference agreement. The importance of committee staffs and interest groups in providing such information, and the influence of House conferees' technical expertise in low-conflict conferences, would be an interesting subject for further study. The present discussion is limited by its focusing on high-conflict conferences and by its reliance on external indicators of internal conference behavior. Even so, it suggests that conferences do use analytic procedures to reduce conflict.

Several conferences reflected information-gathering procedures which focused on the positions of extracongressional actors. This type of information may perform the same function as technical information in achieving a conference settlement. Because the cases which demonstrated these procedures were generally high-conflict conferences, and because these procedures are often so similar to those employed in expanding the arena of bargaining, it was decided to include these conferences in the later sections dealing with that subject.

Conflict between individuals in an organization is usually characterized by a great deal of uncertainty regarding various alternatives and a general lack of commitment among organizational members. Analytic procedures help to resolve interindividual conflict by providing information which reduces this uncertainty and limits the number of possible alternatives. Intergroup conflict is characterized as conflict arising from different commitments to particular courses of action. Intergroup con-

---

8. *Congressional Quarterly Almanac,* XXII, 1966, 396.
9. *Ibid.,* p. 230.

flict occurs in a more ordered atmosphere where there is less uncertainty, a limited number of alternatives, a felt need for joint decision-making, and either a difference in goals or a difference in perceptions of reality.[10]

It is obvious that most conflict in Congress tends to be intergroup conflict. There is, however, variation in the way conflict is resolved. Some conferences reflect a structured, bipolar conflict between two unified groups, the House and Senate. Other conferences resemble an interindividual conflict in that differences exist among a large number of groups in both chambers and there is a great deal of uncertainty about alternatives. It is in the latter type of conference that we expect to find analytic procedures employed in conflict reduction.

The effect of such interindividual conflicts on conference interaction is mitigated by the existence of norms concerning the behavior of congressmen as conferees. The apparent consensus on conference role orientations suggests that pre-conference interindividual conflict may be transformed into conference intergroup conflict by a congressman's behavior in terms of his conference role. Such a transformation would lead to the predominance of bargaining procedures in conference interaction.

Conference Role of Chamber Delegate

At the beginning of this study, it was speculated that conferees' representational roles vis-à-vis their chamber might be similar to the delegate and trustee roles of the legislator as representative of his constituency.[11] A conferee as delegate would be expected to defend his chamber's position, regardless of his agreement or disagreement with that position. A conferee acting as a trustee would be expected to attempt to influence the conference settlement in terms of what he thinks is right, on his "considered judgment of the facts involved in the issue."[12]

This study, it should be emphasized, does not measure role behavior of conferees. We cannot say that conferees who verbally espouse a particular

10. March and Simon, *Organizations*, pp. 119–21.
11. The distinction, of course, dates back to Burke, and is discussed in almost all recent works dealing with legislative behavior. Eulau's chapter in John Wahlke, Heinz Eulau, William Buchanan, and Leroy Ferguson, *The Legislative System* (New York: John Wiley, 1962), pp. 267–86, is the immediate source here. The politico role is not included because it seemed to add little to this very general outline of conference representational roles.
12. *Ibid.*, p. 286. The trustee orientation seems to underlie Senator Morse's statement quoted in Chapter III, note 31.

conference role behave in a manner systematically different from conferees who manifest another role orientation. This discussion is essentially descriptive, and is limited to a description of an attitudinal rather than a behavioral phenomenon. Within these limits, we can try to determine whether there exists on the part of legislators some degree of consensus as to the expected behavior of the legislator as conferee. Discovery of such consensus would certainly not preclude frequent deviance from the behavioral norm. It would, however, allow us to make assumptions about expected behavior which might serve as a base for the measurement of actual behavior.

In his study of appropriations conferences, Richard Fenno has observed that there are shared goal expectations in such situations which establish the parameters of conference activity and help to maintain the conference system. Two important expectations are that each chamber's delegation will struggle hard to attain a settlement bill similar to its chamber's bill, and that the conference committee will ultimately produce a compromise bill acceptable to a majority in each chamber.[13]

In the following discussion it is important to keep in mind that conference activity takes place in a setting, not of total conflict but of consensus on the need for cooperation among the conference delegations. Each set of managers attempts to attain a conference bill in tune with the position of its chamber. A limit on this demand, however, is provided by general recognition that the function of a conference is to produce a mutually acceptable bill. A representative comments:

> As in any conference, you must give some and you must take some, and we both did the best we could without counting how many points first one side won or the other side won, but really trying, as conferees should try, to improve the legislation and to reconcile the differences that existed between the two houses.[14]

The often-discussed problem of conference delegations consisting of many members who opposed the legislation in their own chambers was dealt with in Chapter III. In discussions of this matter there is usually an assumption about conference role behavior. A conferee acting as trustee would tend to oppose provisions of his chamber's bill which he had earlier been against. The conferee whose role orientation is that of cham-

13. Richard F. Fenno, *The Power of the Purse: Appropriations Politics in Congress* (Boston: Little, Brown, 1966), p. 617.
14. House, *Congressional Record*, 89th Cong., 1st sess., 1965, 111, pt. 18, 23933.

ber delegate, however, would be more likely to subordinate his own position to that represented by his chamber's decision. Widespread behavior reflecting a conference role of delegate would tend to reduce the effect of representation of nonsupporters.[15]

A review of the conferences in this study suggests that in both houses there is a norm regarding conference representation. It supports the conference role of chamber delegate. Although the acceptance of this role was not measured in any such systematic manner as interviewing congressmen, all legislators' comments regarding conference representational roles tended to support that of chamber delegate.[16] A member of the House describes this role:

> First, I want to point out that I signed the conference report, although I'm going to advocate to my colleagues, those who voted against the bill in the House, that I still feel the bill itself is essentially unsound, and therefore shall vote against the conference report if it comes to a vote.
>
> It is important to explain the difference between the responsibility that a Member assumes as a conferee, the responsibilities as I see them of working out the differences between the House and Senate versions, and the responsibilities a Member has in his primary capacity of representing the people. As a conferee, my responsibility as I saw it was to do the best I could to work out the best version. So I signed the conference report, because in essence the House version prevailed and what Senate amendments were agreed to, with a few exceptions, improved the bill.[17]

The essence of this delegate role seems to be not simply that a conferee supports his chamber's position but that he supports it in spite of his own position on the legislation. The individual legislator's convictions are expected to be subordinated to the larger purpose of obtaining a conference bill similar to his chamber's bill. That the sacrifice of one's own position to the chamber's will is a congressional value is illustrated by the following excerpt from Senate debate:

> This was one of the hardest fought conferences that I have ever participated in, or have seen. It would be most unfair to conclude action

15. The real world, of course, is never this neat. The representational role sector may be subdivided to include roles vis-à-vis the electoral constituency, interest groups, subcommittee or committee, or, in the case of conference representation, one's parent chamber. A conferee acting as delegate vis-à-vis his electoral constituency might find himself in conflict with conferees acting as delegates vis-à-vis the parent chamber. Would he then be classified as a delegate or trustee in that particular conference interaction?

16. Fenno's study also supports this finding of a general norm favoring the conference role of chamber delegate. See *Power of the Purse*, p. 618.

17. House, *Congressional Record*, 89th Cong., 1st sess., 1965, 111, pt. 13, 18391.

without paying tribute to my beloved colleague [the committee chairman], who carried it through not only with consummate skill, but often against his own convictions.

The Senator from Vermont, who joined us in conference, also did great good. There were times when he had to subordinate his deep convictions in order to arrive at a result.[18]

Given the existence of a norm supporting a delegate conference role, we might ask whether failing to support his chamber's bill in an earlier legislative stage would have any effect on a member's behavior as a conferee.[19] As the discussion in Chapter III indicated, many observers feel that a member who did not support a piece of legislation in his own house would be a less than enthusiastic supporter of his chamber's position in conference. Conference support of a chamber position, however, is not simply a dichotomous choice. Conferees are not presented with a simple yea or nay decision, but rather with a continuum reflecting many degrees of support or nonsupport.

The role of chamber delegate is broad enough to include many different patterns of generally supportive behavior. Simply because a conferee acts in terms of the chamber delegate role does not mean that he will maintain a strong commitment to every provision of his chamber's bill. When conference bargaining becomes intense, and when it looks like continued maintenance of the delegation's position might lead to a stalemate, we would expect to see some of the less committed delegates reduce their level of support for the chamber position.

Role behavior which reflects a delegate orientation, then, is correctly conceived not as one single course of behavior but as many different patterns of supportive behavior. One of the factors affecting this behavior is the conferee's status or formal position, and, thus, the level of activity expected of him. A conference delegation chairman may be moved from a position of qualified to intense support of the chamber position as a

18. Senate, *Congressional Record*, 88th Cong., 1st sess., 1963, 109, pt. 19, 24483.

19. Again it should be emphasized that we are assuming such a legislative norm will affect conferees' behavior. The behavior itself is not measured here, and to be effectively measured would require the researcher to determine each conferee's position on each point of contention and to measure each legislator's actual behavior within the conference itself. This caveat is suggested because of some studies' indicating a gap between legislative norms and actual behavior. For example, see Charles O. Jones, "The Role of the Congressional Subcommittee," *Midwest Journal of Political Science*, VI (November, 1962), 327–44; Ralph K. Huitt, "The Outsider in the Senate: An Alternative Role," *American Political Science Review*, LV (September, 1961), 566–67; Huitt, "The Morse Committee Assignment Controversy: A Study in Senate Norms," *American Political Science Review*, LI (June, 1957), 313–29.

function of his high level of activity as chairman. Other members of a conference delegation may play a relatively passive role as chamber delegate.

In Chapter IV, we discussed Fenno's suggestion that Senate dominance in appropriations conferences is related to the fact that the Senate conferees draw more upon the support of their parent chamber than do the House conferees.[20] The delegate role is very much a part of this relationship between conferees and their chamber. If influence in conference depends upon the supportive relationship between the conference delegation and the parent chamber, a conferee can exercise this influence by maintaining a delegate role. The delegate role provides a conferee, and a conference delegation, with justification for positions taken in conference.

This relationship is dependent on conferees assuming a delegate role and on the parent chamber's providing a policy decision to be represented in conference. The need for both requirements to be met is perhaps best illustrated by considering a case where the second requirement, a chamber decision, was not fulfilled. The Senate, in 1946, had completely rewritten a bill amending the Emergency Price Control Act, which had already passed the House. In considering a resolution to send the bill to conference, one representative commented:

> Personally, I think the conferees of the House are going to be in a rather sad position when they go into conference without any instructions whatever.
>
> They are going to be in a position where the Senators can say, "Well, what makes you take this position? Why do you argue this or that point? The House has not even passed upon this bill. You have no instructions of any kind from your House colleagues. They have not voted upon the issues we are considering here in this conference."
>
> And the House conferees in all honor and honesty, and I am sure that they are honorable men, will have to admit that they do not know what the House thinks about the issues involved, and that they are simply expressing their own personal opinions.[21]

This statement tends to reinforce Fenno's observation regarding sources of conference influence. If a chamber position is lacking, the conferees from that chamber are placed in an inferior position in terms of relative conference influence. Similarly, adoption of a trustee conference role will

---

20. Chapter IV, note 12.
21. House, *Congressional Record*, 79th Cong., 2d sess., 1946, 92, pt. 7, 9130.

automatically deprive conferees of an important source of influence. A clear chamber policy position and conference delegates representing that decision would seem to maximize a chamber's influence in the conference committee.

Many conference bills represent issues which tend to divide each chamber into many groups. As the legislation moves toward passage in each house, we would expect the bargaining process, and subsequent adaptation of the bill, to produce coalitions which would reduce the number of conflicting groups. This movement away from a situation resembling interindividual conflict and toward one resembling intergroup conflict would lead to increased use of bargaining, rather than information-gathering, to reduce conflict.

Even so, there are some cases where the conference conflict resembles interindividual conflict because of the large number of conflicting groups in both houses and because of prevailing conditions of uncertainty and low information. In such cases, general adoption of a delegate role by conferees would have the effect of reducing the number of conflicting groups and further crystallizing the conflict into an intergroup situation. This intergroup conflict would, in turn, lead us to expect bargaining procedures rather than analytic procedures to be employed to resolve differences. Let us, then, turn to a consideration of some of the aspects of conference bargaining illustrated in the conferences studied.

Conference Bargaining: Conflict and Cooperation

The term *bargaining* is commonly used to describe legislative behavior, but it often connotes different patterns of interaction when used by different students of the legislative process.[22] Most discussions emphasize the cooperative nature of bargaining as a process for reducing legislative conflict and arriving at mutually acceptable decisions. Legislative interaction, in Schelling's terms, tends to correspond more to the "efficiency"

22. Some writers tend to emphasize the logrolling, cooperative types of bargaining exchange. For example, see Donald R. Matthews, *U.S. Senators and Their World* (New York: Random House, Vintage Books, 1960), p. 100; and Richard Fenno, "The Internal Distribution of Influence: The House," in *The Congress and America's Future,* ed. David Truman (Englewood Cliffs, N.J.: Prentice-Hall, 1965), p. 73. Others, while recognizing that cooperation and recognition of mutual interests characterize most legislative bargaining, expand their consideration of bargaining to include situations more closely resembling the zero-sum situation. See Peabody, "Organization Theory," p. 3; and Jeffrey L. Pressman, *House vs. Senate* (New Haven: Yale University Press, 1966), pp. 63–79.

aspect of bargaining, exploring for mutually profitable adjustments, than it does to the "distributional" aspect of bargaining which obtains in a more nearly zero-sum situation.[23]

Because of the prevalence of bargaining forms demonstrating cooperation and mutual adjustment and the existence of legislative norms which limit and control conflict, there is a tendency for political scientists to deemphasize patterns of legislative interaction reflecting a greater degree of conflict.[24] Congressional conflict in some areas (e.g., federal aid to education and foreign aid), moreover, is perhaps more correctly conceived as conflict in which one principal's gain is the other's loss.[25] Because of this great variation in the degree of conflict, it is necessary to be quite explicit as to how the term bargaining is being used in a discussion of legislative interaction.

It was noted earlier that March and Simon distinguish bargaining from other conflict-reduction processes in that it occurs when there is conflict over goals as well as means. They further delineate the term by noting that "we can identify a bargaining process by its paraphernalia of acknowledged conflict of interests, threats, falsification of position, and (in general) gamesmanship."[26] In this study, the term bargaining will be limited to those patterns of interaction which demonstrate the exercise of such threats and promises, and go beyond the analytic processes of information-gathering and mediation of subgoals.

Another component of this definition is provided by Schelling's discussion of situations related to the distributional aspect of bargaining.

23. Thomas C. Schelling, *The Strategy of Conflict* (New York: Oxford University Press, 1963), p. 21.

24. This emphasis on cooperation is certainly related to institutional mechanisms for controlling conflict which are found in an organization such as the Congress. That such an emphasis may also be a function of reliance on aspects of systems analysis and structural-functionalism is a supposition worth considering. See Pierre L. van den Berghe, "Dialectic and Functionalism: Toward a Theoretical Synthesis," *American Sociological Review*, XXVIII (October, 1963), 695–705; Roger Davidson and David Kovenock, "The Catfish and the Fisherman: Congress and Prescriptive Political Science," *American Behavioral Scientist*, X (June, 1967), 27; and John S. Saloma, *Congress and the New Politics* (Boston: Little, Brown, 1969), p. 24.

25. Peabody, "Organization Theory," p. 3, makes this point in regard to federal aid to education.

26. March and Simon, *Organizations*, p. 130. Distinguishing bargaining from other forms of conflict reduction in terms of the employment of promises and threats is a pattern found in other discussions of bargaining as well. Charles Lindblom, in *The Intelligence of Democracy* (New York: Free Press, 1965), p. 71, defines bargaining as "a form of partisan mutual adjustment in which in a symmetrical relation X and Y each, as a recognized condition of making effective his own decision, induces a response from the other by making conditional threats of deprivation and/or conditional promises of gratification."

Such situations, he observes, "involve an element of pure bargaining—bargaining in which each party is guided mainly by his expectations of what the other will accept. But with each guided by expectations and knowing that the other is too, expectations become compounded." [27] The emphasis here is on continuous interaction in which both parties act in terms of anticipated reactions. Bargaining, as used here, refers neither to a simple behavior pattern in which one actor structures his demands in terms of anticipated reactions of the other, nor to behavior which is not the result of direct interchange between two or more actors.[28] Rather, the type of bargaining being considered is a dynamic process in which both actors are guided by changing mutual expectations of what the other will accept. The expectations and the change are a result of inter-action.

Behavior guided by expectations and the employment of threats and promises suggest a final delineation of bargaining activity in conference interaction: its indeterminacy. In the type of bargaining situations under consideration, it is assumed that "there is some range of alternative outcomes in which any point is better for both sides than no agreement at all." [29] In order to achieve a favorable bargaining decision, each side runs the risk of miscalculating the intentions and commitments of the other, thus effecting a stalemate. Because of incomplete information regarding the expectations of the other, one actor, in attempting to maximize his bargaining payoff, may produce a breakdown of the bargaining process, making it impossible to achieve a decision. Mancur Olson has suggested that the risk of miscalculation is present even in the type of low-conflict bargaining represented by the legislative logroll:

> Unless he is willing to vote for the legislation desired by the others, the particular special interest legislator in question will not be able to get his own legislation passed. So his goal would be to work out a coalition with other special interest legislators in which they would vote for exactly the legislation he wanted, and he in turn would give them as little in return as possible, by insisting that they moderate their legislative demands.
> But since every potential logroller has the same strategy, the result is indeterminate: the logs may be rolled, or they may not. Every one of the

27. Schelling, *Strategy of Conflict*, p. 21.
28. Lewis Froman discusses a type of bargaining which he refers to as anticipated reaction. This bargaining type differs from that considered here primarily in Froman's anticipated reaction being a non-negotiated bargaining, one in which there is no actual interchange between the bargaining parties.
29. Schelling, *Strategy of Conflict*, p. 22.

interests will be better off if the logrolling is done than if it is not, but as individual interests strive for better legislative bargains the result of the competing strategies may be that no agreement is reached.[30]

In summary, the type of conference interaction considered here is characterized by behavior structured in terms of changing mutual expectations, the employment of threats and promises, and a degree of indeterminacy and risk. Variation in the degree of conflict represented by different conferences is recognized, but most conferences are correctly perceived not as zero-sum games but rather as patterns of interaction in which "mutual dependence is part of the logical structure and demands some kind of collaboration or mutual accommodation."[31]

The discussion in this chapter is organized in terms of strategies outlined by Thomas Schelling.[32] Not only did Schelling's approach lend coherence to the subject, but also it suggested strategies which had not been considered previously and were found to pertain to some of the conferences studied.

The interaction surrounding one particular conference will often demonstrate many different bargaining strategies. It should again be emphasized that in the discussion which follows we are concerned more with describing general patterns of conference bargaining than with providing complete descriptions of bargaining interaction involved in particular conferences.

Strength through Commitment and Commitment through Instructions

Schelling notes that most bargaining tactics share the characteristic of strengthening one's position by limiting one's own alternatives. "The essence of these tactics," he suggests, "is some voluntary, but irreversible sacrifice of freedom of choice. They rest on the paradox that the power to constrain an adversary may depend on the power to bind oneself."[33]

30. Mancur Olson, Jr., *The Logic of Collective Action* (Cambridge: Harvard University Press, 1965), p. 43, n. 64.
31. Schelling, *Strategy of Conflict*, p. 83.
32. The bargaining strategies are those presented in Schelling's second chapter, "An Essay on Bargaining," in *Strategy of Conflict*. Although conference bargaining more closely resembles the cooperative games discussed in Chapters Four and Five, strategies outlined in this earlier chapter of zero-sum games did correspond to many elements of conference bargaining.
33. *Ibid.*, p. 22.

Although Schelling's analysis contradicts the assumption that flexibility in a bargaining situation is a desired value of the agents concerned, it is not a completely new assertion unrelated to statements by other political analysts. E. E. Schattschneider has asserted that "the definition of alternatives is the supreme instrument of power." [34] Influencing the number of alternatives may alter the conflict in favor of one or another party. Schelling's tactics reflect this general exercise of power through reducing the number of alternatives. The actor who sacrifices flexibility by effecting the removal of one or more alternatives may increase his bargaining power.

One party in a bargaining situation may increase its power by clearly demonstrating to the other side that it is limited in the possible alternatives which it may consider by "instructions that are difficult or impossible to change, such instructions (and their inflexibility) being visible to the opposite party." [35] These instructions come from outside the immediate bargaining system and are not a part of the negotiations.

Conferees following such a tactic may ask the parent chamber for a vote instructing them to uphold the chamber position on a particular matter. This enables conferees to remove a particular alternative from the negotiating agenda. The probability of achieving a favorable result on this particular provision is increased by demonstrating an inflexible commitment to the parent chamber's position. Jeffrey Pressman, in citing cases where such a tactic was employed, notes: "By committing themselves to a position and by showing that 'even if we did surrender, our house wouldn't accept the bill,' a group of conferees can gain a powerful bargaining advantage." [36]

Instruction of a chamber's delegation, however, is not a common pattern of conference bargaining. In spite of the fact that such a tactic obviously strengthens one's bargaining position, instruction is considered an unusual procedure in both houses. Richard Fenno suggests that one reason for this is the existence of joint chamber expectations prescribing compromise. Although such norms do not preclude the exercise of threats "inside the conference room, the threat of one group to seek instructions from the parent chamber is considered the ultimate weapon." [37]

34. Schattschneider, *Semi-Sovereign People*, p. 68.
35. Schelling, *Strategy of Conflict*, p. 29.
36. Pressman, *House vs. Senate*, p. 67.
37. Fenno, *Power of the Purse*, p. 658. David Paletz found a reluctance to employ instructions similar to that reported here. See his "Influence in Congress: An Analysis of the Nature and Effects of Conference Committees" (Paper delivered at the 66th Annual Meeting of the American Political Science Association, Los Angeles, September, 1970), pp. 9, 11.

Employment of ultimate weapons is not conducive to compromise.

Legislators' perceptions of the function of instructing conferees are sometimes quite similar to those suggested by Schelling. By instructing conferees, the parent chamber is acting to remove from the shoulders of its own delegation the burden of negotiating a particular difference. A representative seeking recommital with instructions illustrates such an understanding of this tactic's function in observing:

> What I am trying to do is to take the distinguished chairman of the committee, and others who will serve as conferees, off the hook by giving them a sound, resounding vote of the House again to back up our position.[38]

But bargaining is not a static process; each side is guided by changing expectations of what the other will accept. Instructions which commit one of the bargaining agents, while they might strengthen that delegation's position, limit its ability to interact in terms of these changing expectations. In the instruction attempt cited above, the House chairman opposed such a tactic because it ignored this dynamic aspect of bargaining:

> So I say to you that in my judgment you should vote not to instruct the conferees because we ought to preserve our ability to meet whatever situations may arise in conference to the fullest extent possible.[39]

Another characteristic of bargaining which limits the effectiveness of commitment through instructions is the indeterminacy of such interaction. A chairman convinced that instructions will lead to a stalemate will oppose such a maneuver because of its greatly escalating the risk of there being no settlement. Debate over instructing House conferees for the Vocational Education Act of 1963 elicited a response by Chairman Adam Clayton Powell emphasizing this risk:

> The gentleman from Minnesota stood here in the well of the House and said as sure as he stands here, you will get aid to impacted areas. Well I stand here also—with just a little more authority—having talked with the Members of the other body all day yesterday and last night, and I tell you you are not going to get any impacted area aid because if you recommit the bill with instructions, you cannot instruct the other body to go to conference.[40]

38. House, *Congressional Record*, 89th Cong., 1st sess., 1965, 111, pt. 2, 2104.
39. *Ibid.*, p. 2103.
40. House, *Congressional Record*, 88th Cong., 1st sess., 1963, 109, pt. 18, 24289.

The "ultimate threat" connotations of instructions, the desire for flexibility to meet changing expectations, and the risk involved in employing such a tactic are factors which make commitment through instructions an uncommon procedure.

Another reason why there are fewer instances of the use of this tactic is the nature of the relationship between the conference delegation and the parent chamber. In Schelling's analysis, a bargaining agent's being given an incentive structure which differs from that of his principal is one means for effectively employing the commitment procedure. However, in conference bargaining there is not just interaction between the conference delegations acting as agents but also bargaining between the two sets of managers and their respective chambers.

This leads to conferees avoiding instructions for reasons unrelated to the interchamber bargaining. To enter the conference room as instructed delegates suggests that the relationship between the chamber and the delegation is not one of support and trust. Two House chairmen comment on this:

> I would very much regret to see the House, on the first appropriation bill of the year, instruct the House conferees even before they have had an opportunity to go to conference and try to work out the differences. I say especially to the new Members that perhaps every 3, 4, or 5 years this unusual type of action is taken, but certainly it is a very rare thing.
> To send us over to conference as second-class conferees, so to speak, would not be wise. The prestige of a group representing the House is to some extent involved. That would be true no matter what committee might be involved.[41]

> I have had a check made and I am unable to find any instances in the past 25 years where the committee on foreign affairs conferees have received instructions. This is a pretty good indication that they have lived up to their obligations to support the positions taken by the House and there is no need to deviate from this practice. I assure the House that instructions will not be necessary to assure its acceptance.[42]

Consideration of conference bargaining in terms of Schelling's notion of commitment through instructions is useful in its delineating one way in which a delegation may increase its bargaining power. On the other hand, the relatively infrequent use of such a bargaining tactic reflects the

41. House, *Congressional Record,* 89th Cong., 1st sess., 1965, 111, pt. 2, 2102.
42. House, *Congressional Record,* 88th Cong., 2d sess., 1964, 110, pt. 18, 23359.

importance of legislative norms of compromise. Bargaining theory may be strengthened by expanding the scope of the situation studied. Dimensions of bargaining between the principal and the agent might be considered as well as the central interaction between agents. As this review of conference interaction suggests, the principal-agent relationship may greatly affect the patterns of interagent bargaining. In the present instance, it leads to bargaining agents' avoiding certain tactics for reasons unrelated to the central intercameral conflict.

Pledging One's Reputation

Another means of strengthening one's bargaining position through commitment is pledging one's reputation. If one agent is able publicly to stake either his bargaining or his general reputation on a particular settlement, he has, by limiting his own flexibility, placed concession beyond his reach. An important part of this tactic is the publicity which attends such a pledge, for a pledge of one's reputation made in secret to another party would not serve to commit the agent in the same way.[43]

This tactic represents a specific type of conflict displacement in its ability to transform the conflict from one involving substantive dimensions to one involving the insubstantive dimensions of prestige and reputation. As in any such displacement, emphasis on new dimensions of conflict is not a neutral process: One party will usually benefit from such a restructuring of the conflict situation. House or Senate conferees who are able to structure a particular conference in such a way that it becomes a conflict along the lines of House or Senate prestige may greatly alter the relative strength of the bargaining agents. If one house is able to commit itself publicly to the position that concession on a specific issue is a matter of chamber prestige, the original bargaining conflict is greatly altered.

At times this alteration represents a strategic choice by one of the bargaining agents, while in other instances it seems to occur simply by accident. An example of the latter, which nevertheless had the effect of biasing the conference settlement in favor of one chamber, indicates that the process of alteration itself carries a value, regardless of whether such a value served to motivate it.

43. Schelling, *Strategy of Conflict*, p. 29.

The 1964 Legislative Appropriations Bill produced an interchamber conflict centering on a provision allowing representatives, but not senators, to send franked mail addressed simply to "occupant." The House wished to permit representatives to send franked material to urban (as well as rural) areas. The representatives claimed that, because their staff facilities were not as large as those of senators, they were unable to compile lists of addresses as their colleagues did. Senators contended that such a privilege would mean massive free mailings for House members in election years.

At this stage, the interchamber conflict reflected the normal tension between House and Senate over matters of elections. A conference report giving the "occupant"-franked-mail privilege to representatives, but not senators, was brought back to both chambers. The reputation of neither chamber had been publicly staked on a particular conference settlement.

The chairman of the House delegation, in discussing the pending conference settlement, was quoted in the *Washington Daily News* as saying, "Nobody on earth can find out names of everyone who is on a Senator's payroll. I personally know of a Senator who keeps two call girls on his office payroll. I know because I've been at parties where they've been." [44] The chairman's remarks were widely interpreted as a threat to name the senator with call girls allegedly on his payroll unless the Senate conferees and the Senate adopted the House position on franked "occupant" mail.

The original conflict between the House and Senate had been displaced to one concerning the prestige of the Senate. Senator Richard Russell articulated such a conception of the new conflict in calling the House chairman's remark "one of the most unexcusable breaches of Congressional courtesy, as well as one of the most massive assaults upon the truth that I have ever seen during my service in this body." [45]

The Senate's reputation was now the chief matter at stake when it considered the conference report, and it rejected the report, two to eighty-eight. Because of the publicity attendant on the conference disagreement and the chairman's allegations, the Senate was committed to a position of rejecting the report or lessening its chamber prestige. The House chairman, in attempting to employ a threat in the conference bargaining, had inadvertently led the Senate to a position of publicly committing its reputation to a particular outcome. In the second conference settlement, the

44. *Congressional Quarterly Almanac,* XIX, 1963, 177.
45. *Ibid.*

Senate's increased bargaining strength was reflected in a compromise closer to the Senate position.

As we noted earlier, conference bargaining represents interaction not only between the two bargaining agents but also between the agent and the principal. Reputation may be at stake also when the conference chairman brings the report back for chamber approval. In presenting a conference bill, a conference chairman will often emphasize his having achieved a favorable bargain. Such a claim is obviously a part of building chamber acceptance, but it also means the chairman has pledged his reputation as a successful bargainer. Consider the following statements by two chairmen:

> I can commend this conference report to the House because in it you will be voting to approve over 95 per cent of the original House version of the legislation. The additions, although numerous by count of amendments, are few in terms of major structural changes.[46]

> Referring to press reports that the compromise version of the base-closing provision represented a setback for the House Committee, Rivers asked: "Does it look like we are losing? I wish we were doing as well in Vietnam as the House Committee on Armed Services is doing on Capitol Hill." [47]

Pledging one's reputation as a bargaining tactic reflects the same general characteristics as other types of commitment. There is the threat of stalemate, and the publicity associated with the pledge helps to give credibility to the commitment. When an agent makes a pledge, he believes that the action will have an effect, i.e., that the other side will react favorably. But again, there is a risk involved. It is unclear, at the time of the pledge, whether such action will have any effect. A public commitment which has no effect on the outcome can greatly hinder one's bargaining influence in future situations.

Continuous Negotiations

The fact that the same set of conferees interact on similar issues over a period of time leads to another aspect of bargaining reflected in conference. Schelling delineates this tactic of continuous negotiations as one

---

46. House, *Congressional Record*, 89th Cong., 1st sess., 1965, 111, pt. 13, 18380.
47. *Congressional Quarterly Almanac*, XXI, 1965, 701.

agent persuading another that the former cannot concede on a particular point because it would lead to an expectation of similar concessions in future negotiations. In order to protect his reputation for future negotiations, he must stand firm in the present case.[48]

Pressman suggests that the effect of such tactics in conference interaction is not necessarily that of a hardening force moving both actors into inflexible positions, but rather a process which permits future repayment for present concessions.[49] Compromise and exchange are encouraged by the promise of future negotiations.

Effective employment of this tactic in conference is demonstrated by one delegation's insisting that a particular settlement in the present instance is a prerequisite to future negotiations. By threatening stalemate, one bargaining agent is able to achieve a favorable settlement. Such a tactic was effectively employed by House conferees for the District of Columbia crime bill in 1966. A Senate conferee explains why he reluctantly agreed to House demands:

> I have signed the conference report on the District of Columbia crime bill primarily because the bill has been a stumbling block to other District legislation. The House District Committee has made agreement on a crime bill a sine qua non of mutual accommodation between the two Houses of Congress on other District matters.[50]

The fact that the same set of conferees represents a stable bargaining system in a particular area may in some cases lead to employment of the tactics outlined by Schelling. One delegation may base its refusal to concede on a specific measure solely in terms of its bargaining reputation in future exchanges. However, given the development of normal patterns of exchange and compromise in such a subsystem, we would expect to see more flexibility and reciprocity over time. Continuous negotiations thus not only provide some justification for inflexibility and high conflict, but also tend to develop norms of behavior maintaining a cooperative system.

Restrictive Agenda

Introducing the concept of restrictive agenda, Schelling observes, "When there are two objects to negotiate, the decision to negotiate them

48. Schelling, *Strategy of Conflict,* p. 30.
49. Pressman, *House vs. Senate,* p. 73.
50. Senate, *Congressional Record,* 89th Cong., 2d sess., 1966, 112, pt. 20, 27286.

simultaneously or in separate forums or at separate times is by no means neutral to the outcome." [51]

A common occurrence in conference interaction ,is the Senate's including nongermane amendments in the bill it sends to conference. When the conference delegation considers the two bills, members of the House delegation may object by stating that their committee does not have jurisdiction in the area of such amendments in the conference bill. Such a maneuver, while limiting the flexibility of House conferees, has the effect of automatically removing these amendments from negotiations. A frustrated Senate chairman describes this procedure:

> Frankly, I have sometimes gained the impression in conference with some of the senior House members that they would be opposed, if they had the opportunity, to the great compromise, even, that brought this Union into being and created the U.S. Senate.
> I have been to conference with a House bill that the Senate had amended, and the attitude of the House conferees was that we had no right whatever to amend it except in keeping with something that the House had put in its bill in the first place.
> When a House committee chairman says his committee has jurisdiction, we can do little about it. Last year we added an urgent amendment to the Sugar Act. We thought it was urgently necessary that the amendment be added to the bill. We amended a Ways and Means Committee bill because we felt it was appropriate to do so, inasmuch as this was a tax measure. It appeared that the House Committee on Agriculture had jurisdiction on that subject. Therefore the chairman of the House Committee objected, and we could not even have the question considered. [52]

House conferees benefit from this structural constraint because it provides them with a vehicle for commitment. Many conference bills pass with nongermane amendments intact. If the House delegation opposes a particular amendment it may use the limit on germaneness to effect deletion of that amendment without having to negotiate. Thus, although the germaneness strictures of the House may reduce the flexibility of House conferees, they also provide an important weapon for strengthening the bargaining position of House managers.

To effectively employ this tactic, House conferees must convince their Senate counterparts that a conference bill including these amendments not only would be subject to a point of order, but also that such a motion

51. Schelling, *Strategy of Conflict*, p. 31.
52. Senate, *Congressional Record*, 89th Cong., 1st sess., 1965, 111, pt. 14, 18503.

would be sustained. In the 1966 Demonstration Cities conference, House conferees objected to the Senate's seasonal housing measure. The Senate's Demonstration Cities provisions were contained in two bills, whereas there was only one House bill. Because the seasonal housing provisions were not included in the Senate bill under consideration in conference, a point of order could be made against adding the seasonal housing provisions to the conference bill. The turning point in conference interaction, however, came when the Speaker indicated that he would sustain such a motion. Senate conferees then agreed to drop the provisions from the conference bill.[53] Thus, the decision to consider matters as a whole or to eliminate provisions for separate consideration can greatly affect conference outcome.

Last Clear Chance

Another means of influencing the bargaining outcome is to structure the situation in such a way as to leave the last clear chance to decide the outcome with the other party. "It is to relinquish further initiative, having rigged the incentives so that the other party must choose in one's favor."[54] This element is a part of the various commitment strategies already discussed. It is worth a brief separate consideration here because it points out the importance of certain structural characteristics of conference negotiations.

Lewis Froman provides an illustration of structural characteristics producing situations reflecting this bargaining procedure in his discussion of civil rights bill strategies. In this instance, the bargaining is all pre-conference and revolves around the question of there being a conference at all. Because conference committee reports are debatable in the Senate and because of the difficulty in obtaining a cloture vote, when the House sends a civil rights bill to the Senate and the Senate changes even a single word, the House is, in a sense, forced to accept the Senate version. The alternative is a conference and another Senate filibuster on the conference report.[55]

Another illustration of the "last clear chance" doctrine is Richard

---

53. *Congressional Quarterly Almanac*, XXII, 1966, 230.
54. Schelling, *Strategy of Conflict*, p. 37.
55. Froman, *Congressional Process*, p. 160. For a discussion of other "last clear chance" opportunities provided by structural characteristics, see Paletz, "Influence in Congress: An Analysis of the Nature and Effects of Conference Committees," pp. 12, 14.

Fenno's discussion of appropriations bargaining. In these conferences, House members typically act on the conference report first. Because of this the House is faced with two options: adopt the report or recommit the bill to conference. If the House adopts the report, its conferees are automatically discharged and the conference committee no longer exists. The Senate is thus left without the alternative of recommittal to conference; it has the last clear chance to achieve passage of the bill. "The Senate, therefore, is under greater pressure at this point to adopt the report. If it does not, the situation reverts to what it was before the conference, a new conference must be called for, new conferees appointed, and the process must begin all over again." [56]

Situations which give one or the other chamber the last clear chance of averting a stalemate, or the defeat of a bill, may be a result of either procedural or temporal constraints. The impending adjournment of Congress or the expiration of existing laws may pressure the second chamber to accept a somewhat unsatisfactory settlement rather than to end up with no bill at all. When one delegation is able to convince the other that the former has relinquished all initiative, it may increase the likelihood of a favorable settlement. A Senate conferee describes how the House delegation was able effectively to employ the doctrine of last clear chance:

> The Senate conferees went to a conference with the House conferees under some disadvantages. Under the procedures of the House it was necessary that we enter into some kind of agreement before midnight last night. Otherwise the conference report could not be considered today and certain excise taxes on liquor, beer, tobacco, and wine would have expired.
> They will expire at midnight tonight unless this report is accepted and the President signs the bill before that time. The House had to file its report before midnight last night in order that it might vote on the conference report today.
> We all endeavored to get the House to agree to the position which the Senate had adopted. However, we found that the House conferees were adamant.[57]

Again we find that the ability to limit oneself is often a source of strength. By giving up the initiative, the bargainer is able to structure the situation in such a way that the other side must choose between a

56. Fenno, *Power of the Purse*, p. 622.
57. Senate, *Congressional Record*, 88th Cong., 2d sess., 1964, 110, pt. 12, 15443.

relatively unfavorable settlement or no settlement at all. Employment of last clear chance tactics requires the bargainer to rely on structural characteristics favoring such a tactic, to evaluate realistically his opponent's reaction to this tactic, and to escalate willingly the risk of no settlement to a point where the outcome is indeterminate.

Outside Influences

Conference interaction of the type we have been discussing does not occur in total isolation. Although most of the strategies we have discussed involve the actions and reactions of conferees themselves, the actual conference outcome may be determined more by the influences outside the immediate conference subsystem. The most common outside influences are the President or executive agents and interest-group representatives.

It is quite common for the President to send letters to conferees urging a particular settlement. In this study such a technique was discovered in many areas. Jewell and Patterson observe that "in recent years, publicized letters to conference committees handling foreign aid bills have become almost a routine tool of presidential influence."[58] Measurement of the influence of such Presidential intervention is a difficult procedure, but at times such intervention seems to be the key factor contributing to the conference settlement.

When we turn to the influence of interest groups in conference, we again find that there is a great deal of variation from conference to conference. In some cases the conference committee will call in executive agency and interest-group witnesses to testify before the committee. At other times the influence of such groups will be more indirect.

An example of such influence is provided in the Voting Rights Act conference of 1965. An important factor in the conference outcome is reported to have been a letter sent by the Attorney General indicating that the proposed conference agreement was strongly supported by Dr. Martin Luther King. This letter was circulated just prior to the conferees' reaching agreement on the bill.[59]

Another potential source of outside influence in conference is the

58. Malcolm Jewell and Samuel Patterson, *The Legislative Process in the United States,* 2d ed. (New York: Random House, 1966), p. 478.
59. *Congressional Quarterly Almanac,* XXI, 1965, 563.

electoral constituency of a representative or senator. Although the employment of such influence is a different tactic in the conference situation, there are cases where it is attempted. In this study, the agricultural appropriations bill of 1948 provided an example of such an attempt. The minority whip in the House referred to published surveys which indicated that a large majority of farmers in the districts of the House committee and subcommittee chairmen opposed the positions taken by the latter in conference. Although one cannot attribute the outcome to this tactic, the final conference settlement was closer to the Senate position than was the first report.

The purpose of this brief section is certainly not to evaluate the relative influence of these particular outside factors in conference activity. It is intended only as a reminder that the previously discussed bargaining tactics do not occur in a vacuum. The outcome of a certain conference is not necessarily settled by one side effectively employing a particular bargaining strategy. The other agent, seeing that he will lose the existing limited bargain, may decide to expand the conflict by appealing to actors outside of the immediate subsystem. Such appeals and their responses may completely change the relative power situation of the conference. The situation again becomes indeterminate and bargaining continues.

A Concluding Note

This chapter on bargaining in conference activity can claim to be neither scientific nor complete. It does not reflect a study systematically measuring the occurrence of particular patterns of bargaining and relating such bargaining to conference outcomes. Nor does it attempt to describe all of the various patterns of bargaining associated with conference activity. Both the nature of the data and the space limits of one chapter preclude such a thorough study. If it has succeeded in more thoroughly delineating legislative bargaining patterns and in relating these patterns to more general bargaining theory, then it has achieved its purpose. Hopefully, it will serve as a basis for more systematic and thorough studies of legislative bargaining in the future.

VI

Summary and Conclusions

In systematically testing the few generalizations regarding conference activity provided in the literature of political science, we have perhaps moved the discipline closer to an understanding of conference activity. We have not attempted to provide an explanation for conference outcomes. Very little of the variation in conference activity is explained; much of it is not even measured. Limits created by problems of measurement have been recognized throughout the study as they have occurred, and we have emphasized the exploratory and essentially descriptive nature of the research. The value of this work lies in its providing a speculative base for further study.

By concisely stating the major findings, we provide a firmer basis for critically evaluating the research. This chapter provides a brief outline of the major findings regarding conference activity in the Congress. No attempt is made to thoroughly review other studies, to discuss in detail the various methods used, or to provide a complete discussion of the findings in each area. For this, the reader is referred to the more complete texts of the earlier chapters.

Party Representation on Conference Committees

Observations have shown that there is a tendency to overrepresent the minority party on conference committees. Such overrepresentation is said to give the minority a strong voice in the important later stages of legislative decision-making. To ascertain the extent of such overrepresentation an index of representation was computed for all of the conferences studied.

Of the total House and Senate delegations, 15% and 17%, respectively, overrepresented the minority party with an index of 1.1 and above. This contrasts with the 36% of the House delegations and 47% of the Senate delegations in which the minority party was underrepresented.

An index of representation was also computed using the standing committee and subcommittee party ratios as a base. This tended to support the finding that there is not a bias toward overrepresenting the minority party in conference.

Party representation in conference generally reflects the partisan division in the committee, the standing committee, and the chamber as a whole. In almost one-half of all delegations studied the minority representation fell within the narrow "representative" range of .90 to 1.09.

Minority party representation on conference committees was also studied in terms of a Democratic and a Republican majority. A Democratic majority tends to reflect the party divisions in the House and Senate, with over one-half of such conferences accurately reflecting Republican strength in the chamber. Every conference during a Republican Congress, however, underrepresented the Democratic minority. The mean index of minority representation in the House is .86 for a Republican majority, and 1.01 when the Democrats are in control. In the Senate, the means are .81 in a Republican Congress, and 1.03 in a Democratic Congress. A difference-of-means test shows the differences in both houses to be significant at the .001 level.

By interpreting party representation on conference committees as a reflection of the effectiveness of party leadership, we may conclude, on the basis of these findings, that a Republican majority in Congress exercises more effective control over conference representation than does a Democratic majority. Such an interpretation coincides with Malcolm Jewell and Samuel Patterson's findings of higher Republican party unity scores for the period they studied. But because of the limits of measurement and comparability, this finding of more effective Republican leadership must remain a hypothesis suggested by the data rather than an empirically verified proposition.

Since most of the issues considered in this study did not divide Congress along party lines, the question of party representation on conference committees was relatively unimportant in terms of conference support of the chamber's majority position. Most observers fail to distinguish between minority party representation and the representation of minority opinion on conference committees. Many comments regarding party representation are based on assumptions about the positions of party members. To provide a more accurate description of patterns of conference representation, the actual positions of conferees on the bill under consideration were analyzed. Such analysis, we hope, leads us beyond questions of party in conference and indicates patterns of representation which more accurately describe relative conferee support of the chamber position.

Seniority, Bill Support, and Conference Representation

The importance of seniority in appointing conferees has been thoroughly discussed. Gilbert Steiner's observation that a tradition of following committee or subcommittee seniority has not yet developed provided the starting point for this aspect of the study.

The standing committee seniority rank and, when applicable, the subcommittee seniority rank of all conferees was computed for each member of the conference delegations studied. It was found that the appointment of conferees more closely followed committee seniority in 35% of all cases, and more closely followed subcommittee seniority in 47% of the total delegations. When only those bills routed through a subcommittee were considered, the tendency to follow subcommittee seniority became much more pronounced. Of all such conference delegations, 88% followed subcommittee seniority in the appointment of conferees. A strong tradition of following subcommittee seniority, when applicable, in appointing conferees has developed since the time of Steiner's study.

Both Democratic and Republican majorities reflect this pattern of following subcommittee seniority. However, a Democratic majority is more likely to follow subcommittee seniority than is a Republican majority. It is speculated that this tendency reflects a greater degree of functional specialization that is found when a majority party has exercised control over the organization of Congress for a long period of time, as have the Democrats.

Charles Clapp, as well as Malcolm Jewell and Samuel Patterson, observed that reliance on seniority in appointing conferees may often lead to a majority of conferees being opponents of the conference legislation in their respective chambers. To test this proposition, the mean percentage of supporters on conference committees was computed for each conference involving a roll call and contrasted with the mean percentage of supporters which would have obtained had strict committee and/or subcommittee seniority been followed. The mean percentage of supporters actually on conference committees was found to be higher than the number produced by following strict seniority rules. One concludes that the seniority system does not so bind committee chairmen as to produce conference delegations unfavorable to the chamber position.

General patterns of following subcommittee seniority, and sometimes deviating from seniority in appointing conferees, indicate that the seniority system in Congress is flexible enough to permit the committee leadership to exercise control over conference representation. The effect of such flexibility is that conference delegations tend to consist of members favorable to their chamber's position. Earlier observations about the effects of seniority on conference representation do not provide an accurate description of general patterns in both the House and the Senate.

Patterns of One-House Dominance

Steiner found the House to be more influential than the Senate in terms of winning a favorable conference decision, the House being predominant in 57% of all conferences studied. A more recent study of appropriations conferences by Richard Fenno discovered Senate predominance in 65% of all conferences whose outcome favored the position of one chamber. The present research analyzes patterns of relative chamber influence in 297 conferences where *The Congressional Quarterly* reported a conference decision favorable to the position of one house.

Senate influence in conference is found to greatly outweigh that of the House. Sixty-five per cent of all conferences settled closer to the position of one chamber favored that of the Senate. This Senate dominance is consistent for all five congresses studied and for both a Democratic and a Republican majority.

Considering the conferences in terms of policy areas, the Senate is found to be predominant in appropriations (78%), national security (67%), public works and resources (67%), general government (57%), and agriculture (56%). Both houses won an equal proportion of the conferences in education and welfare and in foreign policy. The House won over half of the conferences in the area of taxes and economic policy only (52%).

Relative chamber influence in conference was also studied in terms of the standing committee handling the bill. Senate dominance was again widely distributed over many committees. The only House committees to consistently win more conferences than they lost were Interstate and Foreign Commerce (71%), Merchant Marine (67%), Veterans Affairs (67%), Judiciary (64%), and Interior (57%).

By considering the House and Senate committees regularly supplying conferees in a particular area as intercommittee subsystems, we may consolidate the above findings into an expression of relative chamber influence in these subsystems. Senate predominance obtains in the following subsystems: Aeronautics and Space Sciences, Agriculture, Appropriations, Armed Services, District of Columbia, Finance, Post Office and Civil Service, and Public Works. House influence is greater in Commerce, Interior, and Judiciary. Both chambers were adjudged equally influential in Banking and Currency, Foreign Relations, Government Operations, and Labor and Public Welfare.

Richard Fenno's suggestion that winning in conference is related to the chamber-committee relationship in both houses was tested by relating chamber prestige to winning in conference. Little connection was found between chamber prestige and conference influence, but it is speculated that more precise measures of chamber-committee relationships than prestige might show this to be an important variable in explaining conference outcomes.

In relating the representation of the minority party to success in conference, we found that House delegations which overrepresented the minority party tended to be slightly more successful than those which underrepresented, or perfectly represented, the minority party. The opposite pattern obtained for the Senate, with overrepresentation being negatively related to Senate success. Because the differences in both are small, it is hypothesized that much of the relationship here is a function of other variables such as majority party, the Congress in which a conference occurs, and the standing committees involved.

Relative chamber influence was also considered in terms of the representation of bill supporters on conference committees. The differences here were again slight, and although representation of bill supporters is positively related to chamber success, no strong pattern justifying generalization was discovered.

Conference Bargaining

Organization theory suggests that conflict reduction may take the form of either analytic procedures which produce conciliation within the framework of agreed goals, or bargaining which permits conflict reduction within the framework of goal conflict.

Conference settlements were found to exhibit analytic procedures primarily through the search for additional information. Committee hearings or the promise of hearings were found to be a common means of reducing congressional conflict in conference interaction.

The conference role of chamber delegate effects a transformation of conference conflict from atomized interindividual conflict to a more polarized intergroup conflict. Such intergroup conflict is related to bargaining procedures of conflict reduction. Because of congressional norms delineating the role of chamber delegate, much conference interaction is expected to take the form of bargaining rather than information-gathering.

Bargaining is identified here as interaction in which threats and promises are employed, behavior is structured in terms of changing mutual expectations of what each party will accept, and a degree of indeterminacy and risk is shared by the conflicting agents. By considering conference bargaining in terms of the typology provided by Thomas Schelling, five bargaining tactics found in conference interaction were specified.

Studying conference interaction in terms of the various bargaining tactics employed suggests that legislative interaction may take more forms than those generally discussed in treatments of legislative behavior. The various tactics considered, while being by no means an exhaustive list of possible actions, indicate that more detailed study of legislative bargaining would be worthwhile.

Refinement of bargaining theory should be another goal of detailed study. In considering the tactic of commitment through instructions it was discovered that values independent of the immediate bargaining situation preclude widespread use of this bargaining tactic. Expansion of the scope of bargaining studies to include variables seemingly unrelated to the central bargaining interaction not only provides a more complete understanding of the immediate bargaining situation, but also serves to strengthen the explanatory power of the theory.

Areas for Future Research

Perhaps the chief contribution this study has made is in providing some focus for future studies of legislative behavior. What we have learned about conference interaction palls in comparison to what must be learned before a satisfactory understanding of this aspect of legislative behavior can be achieved.

Generalizations regarding party representation, the effects of seniority, and relative chamber influence have been found to be inaccurate descriptions of actual behavior. Perceived patterns of behavior eliciting critiques of Congress and proposals for reform are sometimes found to be inaccurate. The seniority system may be dysfunctional for the legislative system in some respects, but it is not an inflexible system precluding the exercise of leadership options.

If we are to explain legislative behavior and to evaluate proposed changes in the existing system, we must first accurately describe existing patterns of legislative behavior. This research on conferences is a modest contribution to that first step. Even at the descriptive level much remains to be done. Studies of internal conference behavior and legislative perceptions of winning in conference are required. Development of more refined measures of partisan representation and support of chamber position are a prerequisite to more accurate descriptions of conference behavior.

Only when we have confidently located general patterns of behavior may we begin the exhaustive task of causal analysis. Any attempt to explain patterns of conference activity must first determine what those patterns are. And just as explanation must build upon a reliable descriptive base, so too must any attempt to evaluate conference activity in terms of system needs or democratic theory be based on a thorough understanding of the existing system. It is hoped that the present study will contribute to this process by generating other research which will bring us closer to an understanding of conference activity and legislative behavior.

Appendix A

The Measurement

of "Winning" in Conference

The following excerpts from *Congressional Quarterly Almanac* are presented here as examples of the wording used to indicate a House or Senate victory in the conference committee. The volume, year, and page number are given for reference.

Coded as a House Victory

1. "The Senate conferees accepted the bill substantially as it had passed the House" (II, 1946, 94).

2. "The conference report retained the more liberal House pay bill without substantial change" (II, 1946, 338).

3. "A conference committee accepted the House version on most of the controversial points" (II, 1946, 455).

4. "The conference committee agreed on a compromise which substantially followed the House version" (II, 1946, 180).

5. "The conference bill more closely resembled the bill as it passed the House, for the Senate conferees yielded to the House on almost every major point of difference between the two bills" (III, 1947, 344).

6. "The bill that emerged from conference in the last week of the session retained most of the features of the House measure" (III, 1947, 437).

7. "Providing allowances for farm trainees was a major victory for members of the House Veterans Affairs Committee who, during conference, won the approval of Senators who had objected" (IV, 1948, 242).

8. "The bill that President Johnson signed was essentially the bill passed by the House in September, 1963" (XX, 1964, 518).

9. "As passed by the House, S.1153 was basically the same as the final version signed into law" (XX, 1964, 592).

10. "The conferees accepted the House-passed provisions in most major areas of disagreement" (XX, 1964, 432).

11. "The major difference settled in conference was the formula for determining individual quotas under the new acreage poundage system. The House version was more favorable to high yield producers than the Senate bill, and the House language, with some modifications, prevailed in conference" (XXI, 1965, 134).

12. "The conferees accepted most of the House changes in the Senate bill" (XXI, 1965, 906).

13. "In most cases, the House prevailed" (XXI, 1965, 148).

14. "The provisions of the conference version were identical to those of the House bill with only a few exceptions" (XXI, 1965, 340).

15. "The House version of S.1404, which was stronger than that of the Senate, prevailed in conference" (XXII, 1966, 585).

16. "The major conference action on S.3105 was acceptance of a House proviso to prohibit the Secretary of Defense from closing military installations without first advising Congress" (XXII, 1966, 613).

17. "The final version was essentially the same as the House-passed measure" (XXII, 1966, 285).

18. "Final approval of S.2858 came after House-Senate conferees, on August 18, accepted the House version of the bill" (XXII, 1966, 797).

19. "Conferees accepted the House version exactly, with the exception of two minor amendments written into it on the House floor" (XXII, 1966, 332).

20. "Senate conferees conceded to the House version on all major differences" (XXII, 1966, 362).

Coded as a Senate Victory

1. "In conference the House receded from its disagreement, and the conference report carrying the amount approved by the Senate was accepted by both" (I, 1945, 21).

2. "In conference the House accepted the Senate amendments" (I, 1945, 451).

3. "Conferees accepted all of the important amendments proposed by the Senate" (II, 1946, 540).

4. "The House at first refused to accept the Senate amendments, and insisted on the appointment of a conference committee. However, the House conferees recommended that the House should accept the Senate version, and this was done by voice vote" (II, 1946, 477).

5. "The House conferees won all the skirmishes and the Senate conferees won all the big battles" (II, 1946, 514).

6. "The conference report being more in line with the Senate than with the House bill, it was accepted in the Senate without debate or record vote" (II, 1946, 584).

7. "The compromise reported by the conferees was, on the whole, nearer to the Senate version, than to the bill as passed by the House" (III, 1947, 13).

8. "The conference committee reported the resolution in a form resembling the Senate bill more closely than that of the House" (III, 1947, 262).

9. "The principal compromises reached by House and Senate conferees were in the direction of the Senate version" (III, 1947, 235).

10. "The conferees reported the bill substantially as passed by the Senate" (III, 1947, 679).

11. "The conferees recommended that the House accept the Senate amendments" (IV, 1948, 339).

12. "Most of the major Senate changes stayed in the bill" (IV, 1948, 86).

13. "The conference report largely followed the lines of the Senate bill" (IX, 1953, 331).

14. "In most respects, the conferees followed the Senate version of the bill" (XIX, 1963, 451).

15. "The conference report, filed December 15, largely followed the Senate version of the bill" (XIX, 1963, 239).

16. "For the most part, the Senate version prevailed" (XX, 1964, 422).

17. "The conference committee agreed to virtually all the new programs established by the Senate" (XXI, 1965, 379).

18. "The conference bill was similar in most major respects to the Senate bill" (XXI, 1965, 305).

19. "On the most important variations, conferees accepted Senate actions" (XXII, 1966, 202).

20. "As sent to the President, S.3700 substantially retained the provisions of the Senate version of the bill" (XXII, 1966, 802).

21. "Conferees accepted, with minor modifications, the Senate amendments to the House bill" (XXII, 1966, 760).

22. "In conference, the House conferees generally accepted the Senate's changes" (XXII, 1966, 660).

23. "The final version of H.R.14929 was very close to the Senate bill, which provided less money and more restrictions than the House version" (XXII, 1966, 118).

Appendix B
Case Study Sample

Following is a list of conference bills included in the case study sample upon which the discussion of conference bargaining in Chapter V is based. The House and Senate committees handling each bill are also indicated.

79th Congress

S. 380. Federal government, full employment. House Expenditures in Executive Branch and Senate Banking and Currency committees.

H.R. 6064. Selective service amendments. House and Senate Military Affairs committees.

H.R. 5990. Appropriations, District of Columbia. House and Senate Appropriations committees.

H.R. 6407. Rivers and harbors. House Rivers and Harbors and Senate Commerce committees.

H.R. 6837. Appropriations, military establishment. House and Senate Appropriations committees.

80th Congress

S. 938. Greece-Turkey assistance. House Foreign Affairs and Senate Foreign Relations committees.

H.R. 3020. Labor-management relations. House Education and Labor and Senate Labor and Public Welfare committees.

S. 758. National Security Act. House Expenditures in Executive Branch and Senate Armed Services committees.

H.R. 3601. Appropriations, agriculture. House and Senate Appropriations committees.

H.R.   3756. Appropriations, government corporations. House and Senate Appropriations committees.

S.   1774. Aid to foreign countries. House Foreign Affairs and Senate Foreign Relations committees.

S.   2202. Foreign aid, recovery. House Foreign Affairs and Senate Foreign Relations committees.

H.R.   6284. Agriculture, price stabilization. House and Senate Agriculture committees.

83d Congress

S.   1081. Controls, temporary. House and Senate Banking and Currency committees.

H.R.   2828. Indians, Menominee tribe, payment. House and Senate Interior and Insular Affairs committees.

H.R.   7839. Housing Act of 1954. House and Senate Banking and Currency committees.

H.R.   8300. Taxes, internal revenue. House Ways and Means and Senate Finance committees.

H.R.   9757. Atomic Energy Commission. Joint Committee on Atomic Energy.

S.   3706. Subversive Activities Control Act of 1950. House and Senate Judiciary committees.

88th Congress

H.R.   3872. Export-Import Bank, extend. House and Senate Banking and Currency committees.

H.R.   6143. Higher education facilities. House Education and Labor and Senate Labor and Public Welfare committees.

H.R.   4955. Education, vocational. House Education and Labor and Senate Labor and Public Welfare committees.

H.R.   6868. Appropriations, legislative. House and Senate Appropriations committees.

H.R.   1839. Tariff, beef imports. House Ways and Means and Senate Finance committees.

H.R.　11380. Foreign Assistance Act. House Foreign Affairs and Senate Foreign Relations committees.

89th Congress

H.J.Res. 234. Appropriations, supplemental for agriculture. House and Senate Appropriations committees.

H.R.　2998. Arms control and disarmament. House Foreign Affairs and Senate Foreign Relations committees.

H.R.　6675. Social security amendments. House Ways and Means and Senate Finance committees.

S.　1564. Fifteenth amendment, enforce. House and Senate Judiciary committees.

H.R.　8283. Economic opportunity amendments. House Education and Labor and Senate Labor and Public Welfare committees.

H.R.　12169. Supplementary foreign aid authorization. House Foreign Affairs and Senate Foreign Relations committees.

H.R.　15750. Foreign Assistance Act of 1966. House Foreign Affairs and Senate Foreign Relations committees.

H.R.　5688. District of Columbia crime control. House and Senate District of Columbia committees.

S.　3708. Demonstration Cities. House and Senate Banking and Currency committees.

Bibliography

Books

Bailey, Stephen K. *Congress Makes a Law.* New York: Random House, Vintage Books, 1964.

Baker, John W., ed. *Member of the House: Letters of a Congressman.* New York: Scribner's, 1962.

Barber, James D. *The Lawmakers: A Study of Political Adaptation.* New Haven: Yale University Press, 1965.

Bauer, Raymond A.; Pool, Ithiel de Sola; and Dexter, Lewis A. *American Business and Public Policy.* New York: Atherton Press, 1963.

Berman, Daniel M. *In Congress Assembled: The Legislative Process in the National Government.* 2d ed. New York: Macmillan, 1966.

Blair, George S. *American Legislatures: Structure and Process.* New York: Harper and Row, 1967.

Blau, Peter M. *Exchange and Power in Social Life.* New York: John Wiley, 1967.

Clapp, Charles L. *The Congressman: His Work as He Sees It.* New York: Doubleday, Anchor Books, 1964.

Clark, Joseph S. *Congress: The Sapless Branch.* Rev. ed. New York: Harper and Row, 1965.

Davidson, Roger; Kovenock, David; and O'Leary, Michael. *Congress in Crisis: Politics and Congressional Reform.* Belmont, Calif.: Wadsworth Publishing Co., 1969.

DeGrazia, Alfred, ed. *Congress: The First Branch of Government.* Garden City, N.Y.: Doubleday, Anchor Books, 1967.

Evans, Rowland, and Novak, Robert. *Lyndon B. Johnson: The Exercise of Power.* New York: New American Library, 1966.

Fenno, Richard F. *The Power of the Purse: Appropriations Politics in Congress.* Boston: Little, Brown, 1966.

———, and Munger, Frank J. *National Politics in Federal Aid to Education.* Syracuse: Syracuse University Press, 1962.

Froman, Lewis A., Jr. *The Congressional Process.* Boston: Little, Brown, 1967.

———. *Congressmen and Their Constituencies.* Chicago: Rand McNally, 1963.

Galloway, George B. *History of the House of Representatives.* 4th ed. New York: Thomas Y. Crowell, 1968.

123

————. *The Legislative Process in Congress*. New York: Thomas Y. Crowell, 1955.

Goodwin, George, Jr. *The Little Legislatures: Committees of Congress*. Amherst: University of Massachusetts Press, 1970.

Griffith, Ernest. *Congress: Its Contemporary Role*. New York: New York University Press, 1961.

Gross, Bertram. *The Legislative Struggle*. New York: McGraw-Hill, 1953.

Gross, Neal; Mason, Ward; and McEachern, Alexander. *Explorations in Role Analysis*. New York: John Wiley, 1958.

Hamilton, Alexander; Jay, John; and Madison, James. *The Federalist*. New York: Random House, Modern Library, 1941.

Huitt, Ralph, and Peabody, Robert. *Congress: Two Decades of Analysis*. New York: Harper and Row, 1969.

Irish, Marian, and Prothro, James. *The Politics of American Democracy*. 3d ed. Englewood Cliffs, N.J.: Prentice-Hall, 1965.

Jewell, Malcolm, and Patterson, Samuel. *The Legislative Process in the United States*. 2d ed. New York: Random House, 1966.

Kahn, Robert L.; Wolfe, Donald M.; Quinn, Robert P.; and Snoek, J. Diedrick. *Organizational Stress: Studies in Role Conflict and Ambiguity*. New York: John Wiley, 1964.

Lawrence, Samuel A. *United States Merchant Shipping Policies and Politics*. Washington, D.C.: The Brookings Institution, 1966.

Lindblom, Charles. *The Intelligence of Democracy*. New York: Free Press, 1965.

McCown, Ada C. *The Congressional Conference Committee*. New York: Columbia University Press, 1927.

MacRae, Duncan, Jr. *Dimensions of Congressional Voting*. Berkeley: University of California Press, 1958.

Manley, John F. *The Politics of Finance: The House Committee on Ways and Means*. Boston: Little, Brown, 1970.

March, James, and Simon, Herbert. *Organizations*. New York: John Wiley, 1958.

Matthews, Donald R. *U.S. Senators and Their World*. New York: Random House, Vintage Books, 1960.

Morrow, William. *Congressional Committees*. New York: Scribner's, 1969.

Olson, Mancur, Jr. *The Logic of Collective Action*. Cambridge: Harvard University Press, 1965.

Peabody, Robert L., and Polsby, Nelson, eds. *New Perspectives on the House of Representatives*. Chicago: Rand McNally, 1963.

Pressman, Jeffrey L. *House vs. Senate: Conflict in the Appropriations Process*. New Haven: Yale University Press, 1966.

Ripley, Randall B. *Majority Party Leadership in Congress*. Boston: Little, Brown, 1969.

Robinson, James A. *The House Rules Committee*. Indianapolis: Bobbs Merrill, 1963.

Rosenthal, Alan, and Green, Harold. *Government of the Atom*. New York: Atherton Press, 1963.

Saloma, John S., III. *Congress and the New Politics*. Boston: Little, Brown, 1969.

Schattschneider, E. E. *Party Government*. New York: Holt, Rinehart and Winston, 1942.

————. *The Semi-Sovereign People*. New York: Holt, Rinehart and Winston, 1960.

Schelling, Thomas C. *Arms and Influence*. New Haven: Yale University Press, 1966.

———. *The Strategy of Conflict*. New York: Oxford University Press, 1963.

Steiner, Gilbert Y. *The Congressional Conference Committee: Seventieth to Eightieth Congresses*. Urbana: University of Illinois Press, 1950.

Tacheron, Donald G., and Udall, Morris K. *The Job of the Congressman*. Indianapolis: Bobbs Merrill, 1966.

Thibaut, John, and Kelly, Harold. *The Social Psychology of Groups*. New York: John Wiley, 1959.

Truman, David B. *The Congressional Party*. New York: John Wiley, 1959.

———, ed. *The Congress and America's Future*. Englewood Cliffs, N.J.: Prentice-Hall, 1965.

Turner, Julius. *Party and Constituency: Pressures on Congress*. Baltimore: Johns Hopkins University Press, 1951.

Verba, Sidney. *Small Groups and Political Behavior*. Princeton: Princeton University Press, 1961.

Wahlke, John; Eulau, Heinz; Buchanan, William; and Ferguson, Leroy. *The Legislative System*. New York: John Wiley, 1962.

Walton, Richard, and McKersie, Robert. *A Behavioral Theory of Labor Negotiations*. New York: McGraw-Hill, 1965.

Wilson, Woodrow. *Congressional Government*. 10th ed. New York: World Publishing Co., 1967.

———. *Constitutional Government in the United States*. 10th ed. New York: Columbia University Press, 1964.

Young, Roland. *The American Congress*. New York: Harper and Brothers, 1958.

Articles

Abram, Michael, and Cooper, Joseph. "The Rise of Seniority in the House of Representatives." *Polity,* I (Fall, 1968), 52–85.

Anderson, Lee F. "Variability in the Unidimensionality of Legislative Voting." *Journal of Politics,* XXVI (August, 1964), 568–85.

Bibby, John F. "Committee Characteristics and Legislative Oversight of Administration." *Midwest Journal of Political Science,* X (February, 1966), 78–98.

Blau, Peter. "A Theory of Social Integration." *American Journal of Sociology,* LXV (May, 1960), 545–56.

Buchanan, William; Eulau, Heinz; Ferguson, Leroy; and Wahlke, John. "The Legislator as Specialist." *Western Political Quarterly,* XIII (1960), 636–51.

Congressional Quarterly Almanac, Vols. I–XXII, 1945–1966.

Davidson, Roger, and Kovenock, David. "The Catfish and the Fisherman: Congress and Prescriptive Political Science." *American Behavioral Scientist,* X (June, 1967), 23–27.

Eulau, Heinz. "Bases of Authority in Legislative Bodies." *Administrative Science Quarterly,* VII (1962), 309–21.

Fenno, Richard F. "The House Appropriations Committee as a Political System: The Problem of Integration." *American Political Science Review,* LVI (June, 1962), 310–24.

———. "The House of Representatives and Federal Aid to Education." In *New Perspectives on the House of Representatives,* edited by Robert Peabody and Nelson Polsby, pp. 195–236. Chicago: Rand McNally, 1963.

Froman, Lewis A., Jr. "Organization Theory and the Explanation of Important

Characteristics of Congress." *American Political Science Review*, LXII (June, 1968), 518–26.

———, and Ripley, Randall. "Conditions for Party Leadership: The Case of the House Democrats." *American Political Science Review*, LIX (March, 1965), 52–63.

Goodwin, George, Jr. "Subcommittees: The Miniature Legislatures of Congress." *American Political Science Review*, LVI (September, 1962), 596–604.

———. "The Seniority System in Congress." *American Political Science Review*, LIII (June, 1959), 412–36.

Gouldner, Alvin. "The Norm of Reciprocity: A Preliminary Statement." *American Sociological Review*, XXV (April, 1960), 161–78.

Hinckley, Barbara. "Seniority in the Committee Leadership Selection of Congress." *Midwest Journal of Political Science*, XIII (November, 1969), 613–30.

Homans, George. "Social Behavior as Exchange." *American Journal of Sociology*, LXIII (May, 1958), 597–606.

Huitt, Ralph K. "The Congressional Committee: A Case Study." *American Political Science Review*, XLVIII (June, 1954), 340–65.

———. "The Morse Committee Assignment Controversy: A Study in Senate Norms." *American Political Science Review*, LI (June, 1957), 313–29.

———. "The Outsider in the Senate: An Alternative Role." *American Political Science Review*, LV (September, 1961), 566–75.

Jones, Charles O. "Representation in Congress: The Case of the House Agriculture Committee." *American Political Science Review*, LV (June, 1961), 358–67.

———. "The Role of the Congressional Subcommittee." *Midwest Journal of Political Science*, VI (November, 1962), 327–44.

Manley, John. "The House Committee on Ways and Means: Conflict Management in a Congressional Committee." *American Political Science Review*, LIX (December, 1965), 927–39.

Masters, Nicholas A. "Committee Assignments in the U.S. House of Representatives." *American Political Science Review*, LV (June, 1961), 345–57.

Parsons, Talcott. "On the Concept of Influence." *Public Opinion Quarterly*, XXVII (Spring, 1963), 63–82.

Polsby, Nelson. "The Institutionalization of the U.S. House of Representatives." *American Political Science Review*, LXII (March, 1968), 144–68.

———. "Policy Analysis and Congress," *Public Policy*, XVIII, no. 1 (Fall, 1969), 61–74.

———; Gallaher, Miriam; and Rundquist, Barry. "The Growth of the Seniority System in the U.S. House of Representatives." *American Political Science Review*, LXIII (September, 1969), 787–807.

Udy, Staley H., Jr. "The Comparative Analysis of Organizations." In *Handbook of Organizations*, edited by James March, pp. 678–709. Chicago: Rand McNally, 1965.

Van den Berghe, Pierre L. "Dialectic and Functionalism: Toward a Theoretical Synthesis." *American Sociological Review*, XXVIII (October, 1963), 695–705.

Vinyard, Dale. "The Congressional Committees on Small Business: Patterns of Legislative Committee–Executive Agency Relations." *Western Political Quarterly*, XXI (September, 1968), 391–99.

Government Publications

U.S., Congress, *Congressional Record.* Vols. 91–112. 79th Cong., 1st sess.–89th
  Cong., 2d sess., 1945–1966. All references to the *Congressional Record* are to the
  permanent bound edition.
U.S., Congress, House of Representatives. *Rules and Manual.* House Document
  No. 374. 88th Cong., 2d sess., 1964.
U.S., Congress, House of Representatives, *The Calendar of the United States
  House of Representatives,* final edition, 79th Cong., 1st sess.–89th Cong., 2d
  sess., 1945–1966.
U.S., Congress, Senate. *Rules and Manual.* Senate Document No. 1. 89th Cong.,
  1st sess., 1965.

Unpublished Materials

Fenno, Richard. "Congressional Committees: A Comparative View." Paper de-
  livered at the 66th Annual Meeting of the American Political Science Associ-
  ation, Los Angeles, September, 1970.
Gilmour, Robert S. "Policy Making for the National Forests." Ph.D. dissertation,
  Columbia University, 1968.
Paletz, David. "Influence in Congress: An Analysis of the Nature and Effects of
  Conference Committees." Paper delivered at the 66th Annual Meeting of the
  American Political Science Association, Los Angeles, September, 1970.
Peabody, Robert L. "Organization Theory and Legislative Behavior: Bargaining,
  Hierarchy, and Change in the U.S. House of Representatives." Paper delivered
  at the 59th Annual Meeting of the American Political Science Association,
  New York, September, 1963. Mimeographed.

Index

.